GEMS OF WISDOM

Words of the great Kabbalists
from all generations

T0130610

LAITMAN
KABBALAH
PUBLISHERS

Compiled by Yaniv C

Gems of Wisdom:

words of the great Kabbalists from all generations

Copyright © 2010 by MICHAEL LAITMAN

Published by Laitman Kabbalah Publishers
www.kabbalah.info   info@kabbalah.info
1057 Steeles Avenue West, Suite 532,
Toronto, ON, M2R 3X1, Canada
Bnei Baruch USA, 2009 85th street, #51,
Brooklyn, NY 11214, USA

Printed in Canada

Library of Congress Cataloging-in-Publication Data

Laitman, Michael.
[Kakh katuv. English]
Gems of wisdom : words of the great kabbalists from all generations / Michael Laitman ; compiled by Yaniv C ; [translation, Susan Gal, Chaim Ratz]. -- 1st ed.
p. cm.
ISBN 978-1-897448-49-6
1. Cabala. I. C, Yaniv. II. Title.
BM525.L253513 2011
296.1'6--dc22   2010042561

Compilation: Yaniv C
Translation: Susan Gal, Chaim Ratz
Translation Assistants: Ronit Ovadia, Ronit Cohen
Proofreading: Noga Burnot
Cover Design and Page Layout: Baruch Khovov
Post Production: Uri Laitman
Executive Editor: Chaim Ratz

FIRST EDITION: AUGUST 2011
First printing

CONTENTS

FOREWORD 9

THE PURPOSE OF CREATION 13
    The Creator Is the Absolute Goodness................. 13
    What Is the Purpose of Creation? 14
    The Purpose of Creation
    Applies to the Entire Human Race 21
    Why Did the Creator Burden Us with Creation? 24
    Why Is the Creator Concealed from Man? 29
    The Creator's Guidance
    Is a Purposeful Guidance 34

THE ESSENCE OF THE WISDOM OF KABBALAH ... 39
    The Question of Life 39
    What Does the Wisdom Concern? 40
    All the Wisdoms in the World
    Are Included in the Wisdom of Kabbalah............44
    Realism and Practicality
    in the Wisdom of Kabbalah 48
    The Wisdom of Kabbalah and Philosophy 51
    The Wisdom of Kabbalah and Ethics 57

THE KABBALISTS..61
  Who Is a Kabbalist?..................................61
  Walking in the Path of Kabbalists..............66
  The Principal Kabbalah Writings...............74

THE LANGUAGE OF KABBALAH 85
  The Wisdom of Kabbalah
  Does Not Speak of Our Corporeal World............85
  The Law of Roots and Branches....................89
  The Language of the Kabbalists
  Is a Language of Branches 95
  All the Languages Are Included
  in the Wisdom of Kabbalah 98

THE CONCEALED TORAH
AND THE REVEALED TORAH 101
  Attainment of the Torah Begins with Sod [Secret]
  and Ends with Peshat [Literal]....................101
  Studying the Concealed Torah
  Is Preferable to the Revealed Torah..............104

WHO IS SUITABLE FOR STUDYING KABBALAH .. 111
  Concerning the Obligation of Each Person
  to Study the Wisdom of Kabbalah.................111
  The Opposition to the Study
  of the Wisdom of Kabbalah 129
  Engaging in Kabbalah
  Requires No Preliminary Excellence 138

The Meaning of Israel
and the Nations of the World 143
   Yasher-El [Straight to the Creator]...................... 143
   Why Was the Torah Given to Israel?.................. 144
   All of Israel Are Responsible for One Another .. 149
   Israel's Role Toward the World 153
   Israel Must Carry Out
   Their Role toward the World 162

Kabbalah Now 167
   Proof that Our Generation
   Has Reached the Days of the Messiah.................167
   An Opportunity for Redemption 174
   The Importance of Disseminating
   the Wisdom of Kabbalah...............................178

The Book of Zohar 185
   Rabbi Shimon Bar-Yochai and His Friends......... 185
   The Importance of The Book of Zohar................187

Torah and Mitzvot 199
   Torah.. 199
   Mitzvot 200
   The Essence of the Work in Torah and Mitzvot . 202
   613 Suggestions and 613 Deposits........................ 207
   The Torah Develops
   the Recognition of Evil in a Person.....................213
   What Is a Prayer?...219
   Only the Light in the Torah Reforms the Person...234
   Workers of the Creator
   Who Make the Torah Arid................................. 242

THE APPROACH TO STUDYING
THE WISDOM OF KABBALAH 255
  The Remedy in the Engagement
  in the Wisdom of Kabbalah 255
  The Importance of the Preparation
  for the Study 258
  The Importance of the Intention
  during the Study 261

FROM LOVE OF OTHERS
TO LOVE OF THE CREATOR 269
  Love of Others Is the Means
  to Attain the Love of the Creator 269
  A Prayer of Many 277

THE NATURE OF MAN
AND THE NATURE OF THE CREATOR 283
  Man's Essence Is the Will to Receive 283
  Egoism Is Embedded in the Nature
  of Every Person 286
  The Superiority of Man to the Beast 290
  The Subject of the Purpose of Creation Is Man....298
  The Discrepancy between Man's Nature and
  the Nature of the Creator 301
  Remoteness from the Creator
  Is the Reason for all Suffering 303
  Two Ways to Discover the Wholeness 308

FREEDOM OF CHOICE 315
   Does a Person Have Free Choice? 315
   The Influence of the Environment on a Person ... 321
   The Freedom of the Collective and
   the Freedom of the Individual Are One 329

SPIRITUAL WORK IN THE GROUP 341
   The Purpose of Society 341
   Obtaining the Greatness of the Creator
   through the Environment..................................... 342
   Unity of the Friends 347
   The Power in Bonding... 356
   Principles of Spiritual Work in the Group 360
   Writers' Envy Increases Wisdom.......................... 366
   The Right Conduct at the Assembly of Friends . 368

PERCEPTION OF REALITY............................... 373
   Everything Is Preordained 373
   The Entire Reality Is Contained within Man 377
   We Have Neither Attainment Nor Perception
   of any Matter... 380
   All Changes Are in the Desire, Not in the Light... 384
   A Thought Is an Upshot of the Desire................. 390
   Time and Motion 392
   Incarnation of Souls 395

The Greatness of Baal HaSulam 399

Kabbalists Cited in This Book 413

Researchers and Philosophers
Write about Kabbalah 443

Further Reading 455

About Bnei Baruch 463

FOREWORD

At the age of forty, Abraham came to know his Maker...

He began to call out to the whole world, informing them that there is one God in the whole world, and He is the one to be worshipped.

He would walk and call out, gathering the people from town to town and from kingdom to kingdom...

Until thousands assembled, and they are the people of the house of Abraham.

He instilled this great tenet in their hearts, and composed books about it...

And the notion was growing and intensifying among the sons of Jacob and their company.

Thus, a nation that knew the Creator was born to the world.

Maimonides, *Mishneh Torah*, "Laws of Idolatry"

Through the millennia, Kabbalists have bequeathed us with numerous writings. In their compositions, they have laid out a structured method that can lead, step by step, unto a world of eternity and wholeness.

Gems of wisdom is a collection of selected excerpts from the writings of the greatest Kabbalists from all generations, with particular emphasis on the writings of Rav Yehuda Leib HaLevi Ashlag (Baal HaSulam), author of the *Sulam* [Ladder] commentary of *The Book of Zohar*.

The sections have been arranged by topics, to provide the broadest view possible on each topic. For smoother reading, slight alterations of spelling and punctuation have been made. In addition, sections originally written in Aramaic and other foreign languages were translated into Hebrew.

We are certain that this book will be a useful guide to any person desiring spiritual advancement, and will lead us all towards a new and better world.

The Editor

THE PURPOSE OF CREATION

The Creator Is the Absolute Goodness

And because we realize that the Creator is, in and of Himself, complete and needs no one to help Him to completion, since He precedes everything, it is therefore clear that He does not have any will to receive. And because He has no will to receive, He is fundamentally devoid of a desire to harm anyone; it is as simple as that.

Furthermore, it is completely agreeable to our mind as the first concept, that He possesses a desire to bestow goodness upon others, meaning to His creatures. And that is evidently shown by the great Creation that He has created and set before our eyes. For in this world there are beings that necessarily experience either a good feeling or a bad one, and that feeling necessarily comes to them from the Creator. And once it is absolutely clear that there is no aim to harm in the nature of the Creator, it necessitates that the creatures receive only goodness from Him, for He has created them only to bestow upon them.

Thus we learn that He has only a desire to bestow goodness, and it is utterly impossible that any harmfulness might be in His domain, which could emit from Him. Hence we have defined Him as "The Absolute Good."

Baal HaSulam "The Essence of Religion and Its Purpose"

What Is the Purpose of Creation?

Man is the center of Creation.

Baal HaSulam, "Introduction to the Book of Zohar," Item 18

The purpose of the creation, of all the worlds, was for man alone.

Baal HaSulam, "Introduction to the Book of Zohar," 39

The Creator's desired goal for the Creation He had created is to bestow upon His creatures, so they would know His truthfulness and greatness, and receive all the delight and pleasure He had prepared for them.

Baal HaSulam, "Introduction to the Book of Zohar," 39

All the conducts of Creation, in its every corner, inlet, and outlet, are completely pre-arranged for the purpose of nurturing the human species from its midst, to improve its qualities until it can sense Godliness as one feels one's friend. These ascensions are like rungs of a ladder, arranged degree-by-degree until it is completed and achieves its purpose.

Baal HaSulam "The Essence of Religion and Its Purpose"

What was the purpose for which the Creator created this lot? Indeed, it is to elevate him to a Higher and more important degree, to feel his God like the human sensation, which is already given to him. And as one knows and feels one's friend's wishes, so will he learn the ways of the Creator.

Baal HaSulam, "The Teaching of the Kabbalah and Its Essence"

The aim of the Creator from the time He created His Creation is to reveal His Godliness to others. This is because the revelation of His Godliness reaches the creature as pleasant bounty that is ever growing until it reaches the desired measure.

And by that, the lowly rise with true recognition and become a chariot to Him, and to cleave unto Him, until they reach their final completion: "Neither has the eye seen a God beside thee"

Baal HaSulam, "The Giving of the Torah," Item 6

Man's reality is built with profound, endless wisdom. The Creator created many a great creature, higher than high and higher still, and all are needed in their posts, for nothing is superfluous and all is based on the fundamental cornerstone, which is that what the Creator desires of man's work is for him to correct all of the deficiencies of creation, and elevate himself, elevation by elevation, until he cleaves to His holiness. There is where all issues of remoteness from Him are found, as well as all their generations, and all the matters in nearing Him and all their generations. Indeed, they are all great and profound matters and all are bound to incarnate under great circumstances to achieve the inclusive wholeness.

Ramchal, *Daat Tevunot (Knowledge of Intelligence)*

Man was made to lift up the Heavens.

Rabbi Menachem Mendel of Kotzk

The purpose of Creation is invaluable, for a tiny spark such as a person's soul can rise in its attainment Higher than the ministering angels.

Baal HaSulam, "A Handmaid that Is Heir to Her Mistress"

The purpose of the creation of the world is the revelation of His Kingdom, for there is no king without a nation.

Rabbi Shneor Zalman of Liadi, *The Tanya*, "*Shaar HaYehud VeHa'Emuna* [*Gate of Unification and Faith*]," Chapter 7

Our final aim is to be qualified for adhesion with Him—for Him to reside within us.

Baal HaSulam "The Essence of Religion and Its Purpose"

The purpose of the soul when it comes in the body is to attain returning to its root and to cleave unto Him, while clothed in the body, as it is written, "To love the Lord your God, to walk in all His ways and to cleave unto Him."

Baal HaSulam, "Letters," Letter no. 17

Every person is obliged to attain the root of his soul.

Baal HaSulam, "The Acting Mind"

It turns out that the purpose of the whole Creation is that the lowly creatures will be able, by keeping Torah and *Mitzvot*, to rise ever upward, ever developing, until they are rewarded with *Dvekut* with their Creator.

Baal HaSulam, "The Giving of the Torah," Item 6

The meaning of the souls of the children of Israel is that they are a part of God Above. The soul cascaded by way of cause and consequence and descended degree-by-degree until it became suitable to come into this world and clothe the filthy corporeal body.

By keeping the Torah and observing its *Mitzvot*, it ascends degree-by-degree until its stature is completed, and it is fit to receive its reward from The Whole. This has been prepared for it in advance, meaning attaining the holy Torah by way of the Names of the Creator, which are the 613 deposits.

Baal HaSulam, "Introduction to the book, From the Mouth of a Sage"

All the worlds, Upper and lower and everything within them, were created only for man. This is so because all these degrees and worlds came only to complement the souls in the measure of *Dvekut* that they lacked with respect to the Thought of Creation.

In the beginning, they were restricted and hung down degree-by-degree and world after world, down to our material world, to bring the soul into a body of this world, which is entirely to receive and not to bestow, like animals and beasts. It is written, "A wild ass's colt is born a man." This is considered the complete will to receive, which has nothing in the form of bestowal. In that state, a man is regarded as the complete opposite of Him, and there is no greater remoteness than that.

Afterwards, through the soul that clothes within one, he engages in Torah and *Mitzvot*. Gradually and slowly, from below Upwards, he obtains the same form of bestowal as his Maker, through all the discernments that hung down from Above downwards, which are but degrees and measures in the form of the desire to bestow.

Each Higher degree means that it is farther from the will to receive, and closer to being only to bestow. In the end, one is awarded being entirely to bestow and to not receive anything for himself. At that time, one is completed with true *Dvekut* with Him, for this is the only reason why man was created. Thus, all the worlds and everything in them were created only for man.

Baal HaSulam, "Introduction to the Preface to the Wisdom of Kabbalah," Item 9

The Purpose of Creation Applies to the Entire Human Race

The purpose of creation applies to the entire human race, none absent.

Baal HaSulam, "The Love of the Creator and Love of Man"

The purpose of Creation lies upon the shoulders of the whole of the human race, black, white or yellow, without any essential difference.

Baal HaSulam, "The *Arvut* [mutual guarantee]," Item 23

The purpose of creation is not necessarily for a select group. Rather, the purpose of creation belongs to all creations without exception. It is not necessarily the strong and skillful, or the brave people who can overcome. Rather, it belongs to all the creatures.

Rabash, *Rabash—The Social Writings*, "Love of Friends"

All the people in the world will connect and be qualified for His work.

Baal HaSulam, Letter no. 55

The Creator desires the correction of the whole world. Therefore, our sages said (*Shabbat*, 88b), "Each and every word of the Creator divides into seventy languages, which indicates the preparation existent in the Torah to complement all the nations.

Rav Raiah Kook, *Meorot HaRaiah* [*Lights of the Raiah*]
"For Hanukah," 87

The whole of humanity is obligated to eventually come to this immense evolvement, as it is written, "For the earth shall be full of the knowledge of the Lord, as the waters cover the sea" (Isaiah 11:9). "And they shall teach no more every man his neighbor, and every man his brother, saying, know the Lord, for they shall all know Me, from the least of them to the greatest of them," "Yet your Teacher shall not hide Himself any more, but your eyes shall see thy Teacher," "And all nations shall flow unto Him."

Baal HaSulam, "The Essence of the Wisdom of Kabbalah"

The end of the correction of the world will be by bringing all the people in the world under His work.

Baal HaSulam, "The *Arvut* [mutual guarantee]," Item 20

Every person is obliged to attain the root of his soul.

Baal HaSulam, "The Acting Mind"

Every person from Israel is guaranteed to finally attain all the wonderful attainments that the Creator had contemplated in the Thought of Creation to delight every creature. And one who has not been awarded in this life will be granted in the next life, etc., until one is awarded completing His Thought, which He had planned for him, as it is written in *The Zohar*.

Baal HaSulam, "Introduction to the Study of the Ten Sefirot," Item 155

Why Did the Creator Burden Us with Creation?

If the purpose of the Torah and the entire creation is but to raise the base humanity to become worthy of that wonderful sublimity, and to cleave onto Him, He should have created us with that sublimity to begin with, instead of troubling us with the labor that there is in creation and Torah and *Mitzvot*.

We could explain that by the words of our sages: "One who eats that which is not his, is afraid to look at one's face." This means that anyone who feeds on the labor of others is afraid (ashamed) to look at his own form, for his form is inhuman.

Because no deficiency comes out of His wholeness, He has prepared for us this work, that we may enjoy the labor of our own hands. That is why He created creation in this base form. The work in Torah and *Mitzvot* lifts us from the baseness of creation, and through it we reach our sublimity by ourselves. Then we do not feel the delight and pleasure that comes to us from his generous hand, as a gift, but as owners of that pleasure.

Baal HaSulam, "The Love of the Creator and Love of Man"

The first rule that we know regarding the intention of the Emanator is that He desires to do good. He wished to create creatures that would receive His goodness. And for the goodness to be complete, they must receive it rightfully and not as charity, so shame would not blemish it, as one who eats that which is not his.

To be rewarded, He created a reality which they will have to correct, something that He does not need, and when they correct it they will be rewarded.

Ramchal, *"Klalei Pitchei Hochma VaDaat"*
(Rules of Gates of Wisdom and Knowledge)

This is the rule: The Creator seemingly restrained Himself, meaning, He restrained His ability, while creating His creatures, not to create them to the extent of His force, but rather according to what He desired and aimed in them. He created them deficient so they would complement themselves, and their completion will be their reward, since they have so labored to attain it. And all of that was only because of His desire to do the perfect good.

Ramchal, *Daat Tevunot (Knowledge of Intelligence)*

The purpose of the whole Creation is that the lowly creatures will be able, by keeping

Torah and *Mitzvot*, to rise ever upward, ever developing, until they are rewarded with *Dvekut* with their Creator.

But here come the Kabbalists and ask, why were we not created in this high stature of adhesion to begin with? What reason did He have to burden us with this labor of Creation and the Torah and the *Mitzvot*? And they replied: "He who eats that which is not his, is afraid to look at his face." This means that one who eats and enjoys the labor of one's friend is afraid to look at his face because by doing so he becomes increasingly humiliated until he loses his human form. And because that which extends from His wholeness cannot be deficient, He gave us room to earn our exaltedness by ourselves, through our work in Torah and *Mitzvot*.

Baal HaSulam, "The Giving of the Torah," Item 7

The primary foundation upon which this entire building stands is that the Upper Will wished for man to complement himself and all that was created for him, and that itself would be his merit and reward. His merit—since it turns out that he engages and toils to obtain that complementation. And when he attains it he will enjoy the fruits of his labor and his share in all his work. His reward—for in the end, he will be the whole one, and will delight in the pleasure for all of eternity.

Ramchal, *Daat Tevunot (Knowledge of Intelligence)*

If the purpose of the creation of the worlds is to delight His creatures, then why did He create this corporeal, turbid and tormented world? Without it, He could certainly delight the souls as much as He wanted; why did He bring the *Neshama* into such a foul and filthy *Guf*?

They explained that there is a flaw of shame in any free gift. To spare the souls this blemish, He has created this world, where there is work. They will therefore enjoy their labor, for they take their pay from the Whole, in return for their work, and are thus spared the blemish of shame.

Baal HaSulam," *The Study of the Ten Sefirot, Part 1, Histaklut Pnimit* [Inner Reflection], Chapter 1, Item 6

Why Is the Creator Concealed from Man?

The reason for the concealment of the face from the people has been explained: it is deliberately to give people room for labor and engage in His work in Torah and *Mitzvot* out of choice. This is because this increases the contentment of the Creator from their work in His Torah and *Mitzvot* more than His contentment from His angels above, who have no choice and whose work is coerced.

"Introduction to The Study of the Ten Sefirot," Item 80

That deficiency was born only out of the concealment of the face of the Creator, who did not wish to shine His face upon His creatures from the start, so they would be complete from the start. On the contrary, He hid His face from them and left them lacking, since here is the Light of the King's face is certainly life, and its concealment is the source of every evil.

However, the purpose of this concealment is not to be concealed. On the contrary, it is to be revealed later and to transform any evil born only out of that concealment. Thus, He established law and order to reveal the face of His concealed benevolence through people's actions. These are the laws and the doctrines which He gave to us. His law is the law of truth, which if a man does, he shall live by them, in the eternal life, for the reward of a Mitzva [commandment/good deed] is a Mitzva. This is the illumination of His face, which He concealed from man in the beginning of His Creation.

Thus, for toil he was created, since the inclination governs him and his evil is great in all kinds of faults, along with his remoteness from the Light of life. And the practice of *Mitzvot* shine the hidden Light upon him until, when he completes his *Mitzvot*, he himself is complemented with them into Light, in the Light of this life.

Ramchal, *Daat Tevunot* (*Knowledge of Intelligence*)

Had he told them about the wondrous things in the essence of the reward, they would necessarily use and assume His work in order to obtain that wonderful reward for themselves. This would be considered working for themselves, for self-love. That, in turn, would falsify the whole purpose.

Baal HaSulam, "The *Arvut* [mutual guarantee]," Item 29

The Creator is surely the epitome of goodness. Indeed, it is the law of the good to do good, and that is what He desired—to create creatures so He could do good to them, for if there is no recipient of the goodness, then there is no benevolence. Yet, for the benevolence to be complete, He knew in His sublime wisdom that the recipients should receive it through their own toil, for then they would own that goodness and they will not be ashamed when receiving the goodness, as with one who receives charity from another.

Ramchal, *Daat Tevunot (Knowledge of Intelligence)*

For the creatures to receive the delight and pleasure, and to avoid shame upon the reception of the pleasure, a correction was made. The correction is restriction and concealment of the Upper Light. This means that before one receives the correction on the will to receive so that it is in order to bestow, there is no disclosure of Upper Light. For this reason, we cannot feel the taste of the *Mitzvot* [commandments] that we keep, which should have given us the taste of delight and pleasure, meaning to avoid the sense of shame upon the reception of the pleasure. This is the reason why there was a correction called "having to aim in order to bestow upon the reception of the pleasure," otherwise concealment lies upon the deeds.

Rabash, *The Writings of Rabash*,
"What Are Holiness and Purity, in the Work"

All is set with ahead of time and each and every soul is already in all its Light, goodness, and eternity. It is only for the bread of shame that the soul came out restricted until it clothes in the murky body, and by its power does she return to her root prior to the restriction, with her rewarded from the whole of the terrible journey that she performed. And the entire reward is the real *Dvekut* [adhesion]. This means that she was rid of the bread of shame because her vessel of reception has become a vessel of bestowal and her form is equal to her Maker's.

Baal HaSulam, Letter no. 25

The Creator's Guidance
Is a Purposeful Guidance

The only tactic is to examine the end of the
act, that is, the purpose of Creation. For
nothing can be understood in the middle of
the process, but only at its end.

Baal HaSulam, "Introduction to The Book of Zohar," Item 4

The Creator is the Absolute Good. He
watches us in complete benevolence without
a hint of evil, and in purposeful guidance.
That means that His guidance compels us to
undergo a series of phases, by way of cause
and effect, preceding and resulting, until we
are qualified to receive the desired goodness.
And then we shall arrive at our purpose as a
ripe and fine-looking fruit.

Baal HaSulam, "The Essence of Religion and Its Purpose"

His guidance over the reality that He has created is in the form of purposeful Guidance, without taking into consideration the order of the

phases of development, for they deceive us and prevent us from understanding their purpose, being always opposite to their final shape.

It is about such matters that we say, "There is none so wise as the experienced." Only one who is experienced has the opportunity to examine Creation in all its phases of development, all the way through completion, and can calm things down, so as to not fear those spoilt images that the Creation undergoes in the phases of its development, but believe in the fine and pure completion of its ripening.

Baal HaSulam, "The Essence of Religion and Its Purpose"

The conducts of His Providence in our world, which is only a purposeful Guidance. The attribute of goodness is not at all apparent before Creation arrives at its completion, its final ripeness. On the contrary, it rather always takes a form of corruption in the eyes of the beholders.

Baal HaSulam, "The Essence of Religion and Its Purpose"

From all of Nature's systems presented before us, We understand that any beings of the four types—still, vegetative, animate and speaking—as a whole and in particular, are found to be under purposeful guidance, meaning a slow and gradual growth by way of cause and effect, as a fruit on a tree, which is guided with favorable guidance to finally become a sweet and fine-looking fruit.

Go and ask a botanist how many phases the fruit undergoes from the time it becomes visible until it is completely ripe. Not only do its preceding phases show no evidence of its sweet and fine-looking end, but as if to vex, they show the opposite of the final outcome.

The sweeter the fruit is at its end, the more bitter and unsightly it is in the earlier phases of its development.

Baal HaSulam, "The Essence of Religion and Its Purpose"

The corrupt conducts in the states of humanity are the very ones that generate the good states. And each good state is nothing but the fruit of the work in the bad state that preceded it. Indeed, these values of good and bad do not refer to the value of the state itself, but to the general purpose: each state that brings humanity closer to the goal is considered good, and one that deflects them from the goal is considered bad.

By that standard alone is the "law of development" built—the corruption and the wickedness that appear in a state are considered the cause and the generator of the good state, so that each state lasts just long enough to grow the evil in it to such an extent that the public can no longer bear it. At that time, the public must unite against it, destroy it, and reorganize in a better state for the correction of that generation.

And the new state, too, lasts just as long as the sparks of evil in it ripen and reach such a level that they can no longer be tolerated, at which time it must be destroyed and a more comfortable state is built in its stead. And so the states clear up one by one and degree by degree until they come to such a corrected state that there will be no sparks of evil.

Baal HaSulam, "The Peace"

THE ESSENCE OF
THE WISDOM OF KABBALAH

The Question of Life

If we set our hearts to answer but one very famous question, I am certain that all these questions and doubts will vanish from the horizon, and you will look unto their place to find them gone. This indignant question is a question that the whole world asks, namely, "What is the meaning of my life?" In other words, these numbered years of our life that cost us so heavily, and the numerous pains and torments that we suffer for them, to complete them to the fullest, who is it who enjoys them? Or even more precisely, whom do I delight?

It is indeed true that historians have grown weary contemplating it, and particularly in our generation. No one even wishes to consider it. Yet the question stands as bitterly and as vehemently as ever. Sometimes it meets us uninvited, pecks at our minds and humiliates us to the ground before we find the famous ploy of flowing mindlessly in the currents of life as always.

Indeed, it is to resolve this great riddle that the verse writes, "Taste and see that the Lord is good."

Baal HaSulam, "Introduction to The Study of the Ten Sefirot," Items 2-3

What Does the Wisdom Concern?

I would like to clarify some matters that are seemingly simple, matters that everyone fumbles with, and for which much ink has been spilled, attempting to clarify, yet we have not reached a concrete and sufficient knowledge of them.

1. What is our essence?

2. What is our role in the long chain of reality, of which we are but small links?

3. When we examine ourselves, we find that we are as corrupted and as low as can be. And when we examine the Operator who has made us, we are compelled to be at the highest degree, as there is none so praiseworthy as Him, for it is necessary that only perfect operations will stem from a perfect operator.

4. Commonsense dictates that He is utterly benevolent, beyond compare. How, then, did He create so many creatures that suffer and agonize throughout their lives? Is it not the way of the good to do good, or at least not to harm so?

5. How is it possible that the Infinite, who has neither beginning nor end, will produce finite, mortal, and flawed creatures?

Baal HaSulam, "Introduction to the Book of Zohar," Item 1

The whole of the wisdom of Kabbalah is only to know the guidance of the Higher Will, why It has created all these creatures, what It wants with them, and what the end of all the cycles of the world will be.

Ramchal, *Pitchei Hochma (Doors of Wisdom)*, Section 30

What is the wisdom of Kabbalah? As a whole, the wisdom of Kabbalah concerns the revelation of Godliness, arranged on its path in all its aspects—those that have emerged in the worlds and those that are destined to be revealed, and in all the manners that can ever appear in the worlds, to the end of time.

Baal HaSulam, "The Teaching of the Kabbalah and Its Essence"

What does the wisdom revolve around? This question comes to the mind of every right-minded person. To properly address it, I will provide a reliable and lasting definition: this wisdom is no more and no less than a sequence of roots, which hang down by way of cause and consequence, by fixed, determined rules, interweaving to a single, exalted goal described as "the revelation of His Godliness to His creatures in this world."

Baal HaSulam, "The Essence of the Wisdom of Kabbalah"

The wisdom one should know is to know and to regard his Master, to know himself, who he is, how he was created, where he came from and where he is going, how the body is corrected, and how he is destined to come to be judged before the King of everything.

To know and to regard the soul. What is this soul within him? Where it came from and why did it come into this body, which is a stench drop that is here today and in the grave tomorrow. To examine this world and to know the world he is in, and for what will the world be corrected. And then he will observe the high secrets of the Upper World, to know his Master. And man will see all that through the secrets of Torah.

The New Zohar with the Sulam Commentary,
Song of Songs, Items 482-483

The wisdom of the truth teaches us the global unity, the side of equality to be found in the whole of existence through the very top, at the parity of the form with this Maker, and how to walk without obstacles by the path of this light.

Rav Raiah Kook, *Orot HaKodesh* (*Lights of Sanctity*), 2, p 393

All the Wisdoms in the World Are Included in the Wisdom of Kabbalah

All the wisdoms in the world are included in the wisdom of Kabbalah.

Baal HaSulam, "The Freedom"

Where the wisdom of researches ends, the wisdom of Kabbalah begins.

Rabbi Nachman of Breslev, *Talks with Moharan* p 225

The greatest wonder about this wisdom is the integration in it: all the elements of the vast reality are incorporated in it, until they come into a single thing—the Almighty, and all of them together.

Baal HaSulam, "The Teaching of the Kabbalah and Its Essence"

There is no other wisdom in the world where matters are so fused and intertwined by way of cause and effect, primary and consequential, as is the wisdom of Kabbalah, connected head to toe just like a long chain. Therefore, upon the temporary loss of but a small cognizance, the entire wisdom darkens before our eyes, for all its issues are tied to one another very strongly, literally fusing into one.

Baal HaSulam, "The Essence of the Wisdom of Kabbalah"

As the emergence of the living species in this world and the conduct of their lives are a wondrous wisdom, the appearance of the Divine Abundance in the world, the degrees and the conduct of their actions unite to create a wondrous wisdom, far more than the science of physics. This is so because physics is mere knowledge of the arrangements of a particular kind existing in a particular world. It is unique to its subject, and no other wisdom is included in it.

This is not so with the wisdom of truth, since it is knowledge of the whole of the still, vegetative, animate, and speaking in all the worlds with all their instances and conducts, as they were included in the Creator's Thought, that is, in the purpose. For this reason, all the teachings in the world, from the least of them unto the greatest of them, are wondrously included in it, as it equalizes all the different teachings, the most different and the most remote from one another, as the east from the west. It makes them all equal, meaning the orders of each teaching are compelled to come by its ways.

Baal HaSulam, "The Essence of the Wisdom of Kabbalah"

The inner wisdom, in which there is no deceit, and whose merit is above all other teachings, is the wisdom of truth, the wisdom of Kabbalah.

Rabbi Shimon Bar Tzemach Doran, Rashbatz, *The Book of Rashbatz*, part 2, Item 52

Since the whole of the wisdom of Kabbalah speaks of the revelation of the Creator, naturally, there is none more successful teaching for its task.

Baal HaSulam, "The Teaching of the Kabbalah and Its Essence"

Understanding the meaning of the word, "spirituality," has nothing to do with philosophy. This is because how can they discuss something that they have never seen or felt? What do their rudiments stand on?

If there is any definition that can tell spiritual from corporeal, it belongs only to those who have attained a spiritual thing and felt it. These are the genuine Kabbalists; thus, it is the wisdom of Kabbalah that we need.

Baal HaSulam, "The Wisdom of Kabbalah and Philosophy"

They have no scientific solution as to how a spiritual object can have any contact with physical atoms to bring them into any kind of motion. All their wisdom and delving did not help them find a bridge on which to cross that wide and deep crevice that spreads between the spiritual entity and the corporeal atom. Thus, science has gained nothing from all these metaphysical methods.

To move a step forward in a scientific manner here, all we need is the wisdom of Kabbalah. This is because all the teachings in the world are included in the wisdom of Kabbalah.

Baal HaSulam, "The Freedom"

Realism and Practicality in the Wisdom of Kabbalah

The vitality of every spiritual matter is the value of knowing it.

Baal HaSulam, Letter no. 17

It is a grave mistake to think that the language of Kabbalah uses abstract names. On the contrary, it touches only upon the actual. This is our law: All that we do not attain, we do not name.

Baal HaSulam, "The Teaching of the Kabbalah and Its Essence"

There is not a single word of our sages, not even in the prophetic wisdom of Kabbalah, that relies on theoretical bases.

Baal HaSulam, "Body and Soul"

It must be known because we are commanded, "Know this day, and lay it to thy heart that the Lord, He is God." Thus, we must know, and not only believe, but matters should make sense.

Rav Moshe Chaim Luzzato (The Ramchal),
The Book of Moses' War, "Rules," p 349

Kabbalah uses only names and appellations that are concrete and real. It is an unbending rule for all Kabbalists that, "Anything we do not attain, we do not define by a name and a word."

Here you must know that the word "attainment" (Heb: *Hasaga*) implies the ultimate degree of understanding. It derives from the phrase, "that thy hand shall reach" (Heb: *Ki Tasig Yadcha*). That means that before something becomes utterly lucid, as though gripped in one's hand, Kabbalists do not consider it attained, but understood, comprehended, and so on.

Baal HaSulam, "The Essence of the Wisdom of Kabbalah"

The lower is studied from the Higher. Thus, one must first attain the Upper Roots, the way they are in spirituality, above any imagination, but with pure attainment. And once he has thoroughly attained the Upper Roots with his own mind, he may examine the tangible branches in this world and know how each branch relates to its root in the Upper World, in all its orders, in quantity and quality.

Baal HaSulam, "The Essence of the Wisdom of Kabbalah"

Every thing that we do not attain and that has no name and appellation, how can we define it by a name? Any name implies attainment.

It indicates that we have attained that name.

Baal HaSulam, *The Study of the Ten Sefirot*,
Histaklut Pnimit [Inner Reflection] Chapter 1, Item 5

The Wisdom of Kabbalah and Philosophy

Sages of Kabbalah observe philosophic theology and complain that they have stolen the upper shell of their wisdom, which Plato and his Greek predecessors had acquired while studying with the disciples of the prophets in Israel. They have stolen basic elements from the wisdom of Israel and wore a cloak that is not their own. To this day, philosophic theology sits on the throne of Kabbalah, being heir under her mistress...

Kabbalah cannot prove its nature and truthfulness, and no revelations will suffice for the world to know it before the futility and falsehood of theological philosophy that has taken its throne becomes apparent.

Therefore, there was no such salvation for Israel as when the materialistic psychology appeared and struck theological philosophy on its head a lethal blow.

Baal HaSulam, "The Wisdom of Kabbalah and Philosophy"

Where the wisdom of philosophy ends, the wisdom of Kabbalah begins. Meaning, philosophers researched only as far as the wheels, but know nothing from there and above. Even in the teachings from the wheels and below the vast majority of them are bewildered, as they know themselves. The wisdom of Kabbalah begins where their wisdom ends, meaning from the wheels and above.

Rabbi Nachman of Breslev, *Talks with Moharan*, p 225

Understanding the meaning of the word, "spirituality," has nothing to do with philosophy. This is because how can they discuss something that they have never seen or felt? What do their rudiments stand on?

If there is any definition that can tell spiritual from corporeal, it belongs only to those who have attained a spiritual thing and felt it. These are the genuine Kabbalists; thus, it is the wisdom of Kabbalah that we need.

Baal HaSulam, "The Wisdom of Kabbalah and Philosophy"

It must be known because we are commanded, "Know this day, and lay it to thy heart that the Lord, He is God." Thus, we must know, and not only believe, but matters should make sense.

Rav Moshe Chaim Luzzato (The Ramchal),
The Book of Moses' War, "Rules," p 349

But I am not an enthusiast of formative philosophy, since I dislike theoretically based studies, and it is well known that most of my contemporaries agree with me, for we are too familiar with such foundations, which are rickety foundations; and when the foundation fluctuates, the whole building tumbles.

Therefore, I have come here to speak only through critique of empirical reason.

Baal HaSulam, "The Peace"

Not only is it the wrong place to argue with them about their fabricated conjectures, but also the time of supporters of such views has already passed and their authority revoked. We should also thank the experts of materialistic psychology for that, which built its plinth on the ruin of the former, winning the public's favor. Now everyone admits to the nullity of philosophy, for it is not built on concrete foundations.

This old doctrine became a stumbling rock and a deadly thorn to the sages of Kabbalah because where they should have subdued before the sages of Kabbalah, and assume abstinence and prudence, sanctity, and purity before the sages disclosed before them even the smallest thing in spirituality, they easily received what they had wanted from the formative philosophy. Without payment or price, they watered them from their fountain of wisdom to satiation, and refrained from delving in the wisdom of Kabbalah until the wisdom has almost been forgotten from among Israel. Hence, we are grateful to materialistic psychology for handing it a deadly blow.

Baal HaSulam, "The Wisdom of Kabbalah and Philosophy"

Since the day I have discovered the wisdom of Kabbalah and dedicated myself to it, I have distanced myself from abstract philosophy and all its branches as the east from the west. Everything that I will write henceforth will be from a purely scientific perspective, in utter precision, and by means of simple recognition of practical, useful things.

Baal HaSulam, "Body and Soul"

Today our generation has already recognized that metaphysical philosophy contains no real content upon which it is worthwhile to spend one's time. Hence, it is certainly forbidden for anyone to take any spices from their words.

Baal HaSulam, "Body and Soul"

Philosophy loves to pride itself on understanding all the negatives about His essence. However, the sages of Kabbalah put their hand to their mouth at this point, and do not give Him even a simple name, for we do not define by name or word that which we do not attain. That is because a word designates some degree of attainment. However, Kabbalists do speak a great deal about His illumination in reality, meaning all those illuminations they have actually attained, as validly as tangible attainment.

Baal HaSulam, "The Wisdom of Kabbalah and Philosophy"

Philosophy loves to concern itself with His Essence and prove which rules do not apply to Him. However, Kabbalah has no dealings whatsoever with it, for how can the unattainable and imperceptible be defined?

Baal HaSulam, "The Wisdom of Kabbalah and Philosophy"

The Wisdom of Kabbalah and Ethics

Many are mistaken and compare our Torah to ethics. But that has come to them because they have never tasted religion in their lives. I call upon them: "Taste and see that the Lord is good." It is true that both ethics and religion aim at one thing—to raise man above the filth of the narrow self-love and bring him to the heights of love-of-others.

But still, they are as remote one from the other as the distance between the Thought of the Creator and the thought of people. For religion extends from the Thoughts of the Creator, and ethics comes from thoughts of flesh and blood and from the experiences of their lives. Hence, there is an evident difference between them, both in practical aspects and in the final aim.

Baal HaSulam, "The Essence of Religion and Its Purpose"

The recognition of good and evil that develops in us through ethics, as we use it, is relative to the success of the society.

With religion, however, the recognition of good and evil that develops in us, as we use it, is relative to the Creator alone, that is, from the disparity of form from the Maker, to equivalence of form with Him, which is called *Dvekut* (adhesion).

Baal HaSulam, "The Essence of Religion and Its Purpose"

The goal of ethics is the well-being of society from the perspective of practical reason, derived from life's experiences. But in the end, that goal does not promise its follower any elevation above the boundaries of nature. Hence, this goal is still subject to criticism, for who can prove to an individual the extent of his benefit in such a conclusive manner that he will be compelled to even slightly diminish his own self in favor of the well-being of society?

The religious goal, however, promises the well-being of the individual who follows it, as we have already shown that when one comes to love others, he is in direct *Dvekut*, which is equivalence of form with the Maker, and along with it man passes from his narrow world, filled with pain and impediments, to an eternal and broad world of bestowal upon the Lord and upon the people.

Baal HaSulam, "The Essence of Religion and Its Purpose"

Following the ethics is supported by the favor of people, which is like a rent that finally pays off. And when man grows accustomed to this work, he will not be able to ascend in degrees of ethics, for he will now be used to such work that is well rewarded by society, which pays for his good deeds.

Yet, by observing Torah and *Mitzvot* in order to please his Maker, without any reward, he climbs the rungs of ethics precisely to the extent that he pursues it, since there is no payment on his path. And each penny is added to a great account. And finally he acquires a second nature, which is bestowal upon others without any self-gratification, except for the bare necessities of his life.

Baal HaSulam, "The Essence of Religion and Its Purpose"

THE KABBALISTS

Who Is a Kabbalist?

The Kabbalists attain a complete thing. Meaning, they are rewarded with attaining all of those degrees existing in reality, attainable to man, and then it is considered that they have attained a complete thing, and that complete thing is called, "a soul."

Baal HaSulam, "The Meaning of Conception and Birth"

Anyone receiving the abundance from the Creator is glorified with the crowns of the Creator. And one who is rewarded with feeling, during the fact, how the Creator is glorified with him, for having found him ready to receive His abundance, he is called "a Kabbalist."

Baal HaSulam, Letter 46

The wisdom of truth is conditioned by all the teachings, and all the teachings are conditioned by it. This is why we do not find a single genuine Kabbalist without comprehensive knowledge in all the teachings of the world, since they acquire them from the wisdom of truth itself, as they are included in it.

Baal HaSulam, "The Teaching of the Kabbalah and Its Essence"

The depths of the Divine secrets simply cannot be comprehended by scrutinizing them with the human intellect, but rather by the Kabbalah, through wondrous people, whose soul has been imbued with the Divine Light.

Rav Raiah Kook, *Orot HaKodesh* (*Lights of Sanctity*) Vol. 1, 85

The truly righteous can perceive the purpose of the next world with their minds.

Rabbi Nachman of Breslev, *Collection of The Moharan*, "Torah," 18

Were it not for sages, people would not know what is the law and what are the commandments of the Creator, and there would be no difference between the spirit of man and the spirit of a beast.

The Book of Zohar (with the *Sulam* [Ladder] Commentary),
Shemot [Exodus], Item 84

The secrets of the Torah will not be revealed to people by means of their material study, but through Divine abundance, imparted from the height of His holiness by His emissaries and angels or by Prophet Elijah.

The Writings of the Ari, The Tree of Life,
Introduction of Rav Chaim Vital to *Gate to Introduction*

The souls of the great righteous sages encompass everything: They have all the good and evil of everything. They suffer torments for all and receive pleasure from all, as they transform the evil of all into good.

Rav Raiah Kook, *Orot HaKodesh (Lights of Sanctity)*, 3, p 153

Understanding the meaning of the word, "spirituality," has nothing to do with philosophy. This is because how can they discuss something that they have never seen or felt? What do their rudiments stand on?

If there is any definition that can tell spiritual from corporeal, it belongs only to those who have attained a spiritual thing and felt it. These are the genuine Kabbalists; thus, it is the wisdom of Kabbalah that we need.

Baal HaSulam, "The Wisdom of Kabbalah and Philosophy"

The merit of one who has been rewarded with cleaving unto Him once more. It means that he has been rewarded with equivalence of form with the Creator by inverting the will to receive, imprinted in him through the power in Torah and *Mitzvot*. This was the very thing that separated him from His Essence, and turned it into a will to bestow. And all of one's actions are only to bestow and benefit others, as he has equalized his form with the Maker. It follows that one is just like the organ that was once cut off from the body and has been reunited with the body: it knows the thoughts of the rest of the body once again, just as it did prior to the separation from the body.

The soul is like that, too: after it has acquired equivalence with Him, it knows His Thoughts once more, as it knew prior to the separation from Him due to the will-to-receive's disparity of form. Then the verse, "know thou the God of thy father," lives in him, as then one is rewarded with complete knowledge, which is Godly knowledge. Also, one is rewarded with all the secrets of the Torah, as His Thoughts are the secrets of the Torah.

Baal HaSulam, "A Speech for the Completion of The Zohar"

Indeed, there is no generation without chosen ones who have been instilled with the spirit of holiness. Elijah the prophet was revealed to them and teaches them the secrets of this law.

The Writings of the Ari, The Tree of Life,
Introduction of Rav Chaim Vital

Walking in the Path of Kabbalists

Come and see how grateful we should be to our teachers, who impart us their sacred Lights and dedicate their souls to do good to our souls. They stand in the middle between the path of harsh torments and the path of repentance. They save us from the netherworld, which is harder than death, and accustom us to reach the heavenly pleasures, the sublime gentleness and the pleasantness that is our share, ready and waiting for us from the very beginning, as we have said above. Each of them operates in his generation, according to the power of the Light of his Torah and sanctity.

Our sages have already said, "You have not a generation without such as Abraham, Isaac, and Jacob."

Baal HaSulam, "Introduction to the Book, Panim Meirot uMasbirot," Item 8

All the matters, for we will be lost even in the literal without assistance from the Kabbalists. To them we will bow down, and all those matters will be revealed to us.

The Book of Education, Parashat Terumah

Maimonides has already given a true allegory about that: If a line of a thousand blind walk along the way, and there is at least one leader amongst them who can see, they are certain to take the right path and not fall in the pits and obstacles, since they are following the sighted one who leads them. But if that person is missing, they are certain to stumble over every hurdle on the way, and will all fall into the pit.

Baal HaSulam, "Introduction to The Book of Zohar," Item 57

Hence, a person has the choice of going to a place where there are righteous. One can accept their authority, and then he will receive all the powers that he lacks by the nature of his own qualities. He will receive it from the righteous. This is the benefit in "planted them in each generation," so that each generation would have someone to turn to, to cleave to, and from whom to receive the strength needed to rise to the degree of a righteous. Thus, they, too, subsequently become righteous.

Baal HaSulam, *Shamati* [*I Heard*], Article no. 99

The most successful way for one who wishes to learn the wisdom is to search for a genuine Kabbalist and follow all his instructions, until one is rewarded with understanding the wisdom in one's own mind, meaning the first discernment. Afterwards, one will be rewarded with its conveyance mouth to mouth, which is the second discernment, and after that, understand in writing, which is the third discernment. Then, one will have inherited all the wisdom and its instruments from his teacher with ease, and will be left with all one's time to develop and expand.

Baal HaSulam, "The Teaching of the Kabbalah and Its Essence"

Through adhering to wise disciples, it is possible to receive some support. In other words, only a wise disciple can help him, and nothing else. Even if he is great in the Torah, he will still be called "a commoner," if he has not been rewarded with learning from the Creator's mouth.

Hence, one must surrender before a wise disciple and accept what the wise disciple places on him without any arguments, but by way of above reason.

Baal HaSulam, *Shamati [I Heard]*, Article no. 105

Even though one has a soul, he is not ready to know Him, "Until the spirit be poured upon him from on high." However, one must lend an ear and listen to the words of the sages, and believe in them wholeheartedly.

Baal HaSulam, Letter no. 19

Although our sages and their teachings gave to us in Kabbalah, by that, they are as trusted witnesses, eye-witnesses, and nothing more.

However, they teach us the way they were rewarded with becoming eye-witnesses. When we understand, our wisdom will be as theirs and we will attain a true and real foundation, with an eternal, glorious building upon it.

Baal HaSulam, "The Remedy of Memory"

Since the more developed in the generation is certainly the individual, it follows that when the public wants to relieve themselves of the terrible agony and assume conscious and voluntary development, which is the path of Torah, they have no choice but to subjugate themselves and their physical freedom to the discipline of the individual, and obey the orders and remedies that he will offer them.

Baal HaSulam, "The Freedom"

As far as spiritual life is concerned, there is no natural obligation on the individual to abide by the society in any way. On the contrary, here applies a natural law over the collective, to subjugate itself to the individual.

Baal HaSulam, "The Freedom"

The depths of the Divine secrets simply cannot be comprehended by scrutinizing them with the human intellect, but rather by the Kabbalah, through wondrous people, whose soul has been imbued with the Divine Light. When we study their words, with the proper preparation, internal conjecture comes forth and settles the matters until they are similar to terms that are comprehended by the natural, simple intellect. We should always adjoin the force of the truth of Kabbalah to this science, and then things become illuminating and joyous as when they were given at Sinai— to each according to his degree.

Rav Raiah Kook, *Orot HaKodesh (Lights of Sanctity)* Vol. 1, 85

Since the mind of the world is one, divided among numerous carriers, it turns out that if two people are clothed with the same mind, they think about a single issue. If there is any difference between them, it is actually in its greatness or smallness. By nature, the small surrender before the great. Hence, those fools who think the exact same thought as the sages ponder the same topic as the sages, and unknowingly surrender and unite with the sages, according to the nature of Creation. In this way the entire world becomes corrected.

Baal HaSulam, *A Sage's Fruit, Talks*,
"Permanent Delight and Excellent Enslavement"

While most of humanity is undeveloped, and the developed ones are always a small minority, if you always determine according to the will of the collective, which are the undeveloped, and the reckless ones, the views and desires of the wise and the developed in society, which are always the minority, will never be heard taken and will not be taken into consideration. Thus, you seal off humanity's fate to regression, for it will not be able to make even a single step forward.

Baal HaSulam, "The Freedom"

Thus you see that in spiritual matters, the authority of the collective is overturned and the law of "Taking after the Individual" is applied, that is, the developed individual. For it is plain to see that the developed and the educated in every society are always a small minority. It follows that the success and spiritual well-being of society is bottled and sealed in the hands of the minority.

Therefore, the collective is obliged to meticulously guard all the views of the few, so they will not perish from the world. This is because they must know for certain, in complete confidence, that the truer and more developed views are never in the hands of the collective in authority, but rather in the hands of the weakest, that is, in the hands of the indistinguishable minority. This is because every wisdom and everything precious comes into the world in small quantities. Therefore, we are cautioned to preserve the views of all the individuals, due to the collective's inability to tell wrong from right among them.

Baal HaSulam, "The Freedom"

The Principal Kabbalah Writings

THE BOOK OF ZOHAR

We did not find a single book in the wisdom of truth that precedes Rashbi's *The Book of Zohar*, since all the books in the wisdom prior to his are not categorized as interpretations of the wisdom. Instead, they are mere intimations, without any order of cause and consequence, as it is known to those who find knowledge, thus far understanding his words.

Baal HaSulam, "Disclosing a Portion, Covering Two"

Rabbi Shimon Bar-Yochai's soul was of the Surrounding-Light kind. Hence, he had the power to clothe the words and teach them in a way that even if he taught them to many, only the worthy of understanding would understand. This is why he was given 'permission' to write *The Book of Zohar*.

The permission was not 'granted' to write a book in this wisdom to his teachers or to the first ones who preceded them, even though they were certainly more proficient in this wisdom than he. But the reason is that they did not have the power to dress the matters as did he.

Baal HaSulam, "Disclosing a Portion, Covering Two"

Rashbi and his generation, the authors of *The Zohar*, who were granted all 125 degrees in completeness, even though it was prior to the days of the Messiah. It was said about him and his disciples: "A sage is preferable to a prophet." Hence, we often find in *The Zohar* that there will be none like the generation of Rashbi until the generation of the Messiah King. This is why his composition made such a great impact in the world, since the secrets of the Torah in it occupy the level of all 125 degrees.

Hence, it is said in *The Zohar* that *The Book of Zohar* will be revealed only at the End of Days, the days of the Messiah. This is so because we have already said that if the degrees of the students are not at the full measure of the degree of the author, they will not understand his intimations, since they do not have a common attainment.

And since the degree of the authors of *The Zohar* is at the full level of the 125 degrees, they cannot be attained prior to the days of the Messiah. It follows that there will be no common attainment with the authors of *The Zohar* in the generations preceding the days of the Messiah. Hence, *The Zohar* could not be revealed in the generations before the generation of the Messiah.

Baal HaSulam, "A Speech for the Completion of The Zohar"

THE WRITINGS OF THE ARI

The Ari's predecessors were not given permission from Above to disclose the interpretations of the wisdom, and that he was given this permission. And also, this does not distinguish any greatness or smallness at all, since it is possible that the virtue of his formers was much greater than the Ari's, but they were not given permission for it at all. For this reason, they refrained from writing commentaries that relate to the actual wisdom, but settled for brief intimations that were not in any way linked to one another.

For this reason, since the books of the Ari appeared in the world, all who study the wisdom of Kabbalah have left their hands from all the books of the Ramak, and all the first and the great ones that preceded the Ari, as it is known among those who engage in this wisdom. They have attached their spiritual lives solely to the writings of the Ari in a way that the essential books, considered proper interpretations of this wisdom, are only *The Book of Zohar*, the *Tikkunim* and following them, the books of the Ari.

Baal HaSulam, "Disclosing a Portion, Covering Two"

Indeed, that Godly man, our Rav Isaac Luria, troubled and provided us the fullest measure. He did wondrously more than his predecessors, and if I had a tongue that praises, I would praise that day when his wisdom appeared almost as the day when the Torah was given to Israel.

There are not enough words to measure his holy work in our favor. The doors of attainment were locked and bolted, and he came and opened them for us...

You find a thirty-eight-year-old who subdued with his wisdom all his predecessors through the Genius and through all times. All the elders of the land, the gallant shepherds, friends and disciples of the Godly sage, the Ramak, stood before him as disciples before the Rav.

All the sages of the generations following them to this day, none missing, have abandoned all the books and compositions that precede him, the Kabbalah of the Ramak, the Kabbalah of The First and the Kabbalah of The Genius, blessed be the memory of them all. They have attached their spiritual life entirely and solely to his Holy Wisdom.

Baal HaSulam, "Introduction to the Book Panim Meirot uMasbirot," Item 8

There is nothing in my views or thoughts that is not sourced in the writings of the Ari.

Rav Raiah Kook, *For the Third of Elul 1*, Item 46.

The merit of one who contemplates the words of the Living God, *The Book of Zohar*, and all that accompany it, and the words of the wisdom of truth, is immeasurable and priceless. It is especially so with the clear writings of the Ari.

Rav Raiah Kook, "Who Love Israel in Holiness," 232

In this last generation, whoever does not engage in *The Book of Zohar*, the corrections, and the writings of the Ari, which are truly a life to the soul....should know that the Torah in which he engages is superficial....and he has no life or a part in life.

Rabbi Yitzchak Isaac Yehuda Yechiel Safrin of Komarno,
The Hall of the Blessing, Parashat Ekev, 7

BAAL HASULAM'S COMMENTARY ON THE WRITINGS OF THE ARI AND THE ZOHAR:

Know for sure that since time of the Ari to this day, there has not been anyone to understand the heart of the method of Ari. It was easier to acquire a mind twice as holy and great as the Ari's than to comprehend his method, which has been held by many, from the first one who heard and documented it, to the latest compilers, while they did not attain the matters fully, at their Highest source, and each one confused the matters and mixed them up.

And yet, by a High Will, I have been rewarded with an impregnation of the soul of The Ari, not for my own good deeds, but by a High Will. It is beyond my grasp, as well, why

I have been chosen for this wonderful soul, which no man has been rewarded with since his demise until today. I can not expand on this issue, as it is not my way to speak of the wondrous.

Baal HaSulam, Letter no. 39

Since faith has generally diminished, specifically faith in the holy men, the wise men of all generations. And the books of Kabbalah and *The Zohar* are filled with corporeal parables. Therefore, people are afraid lest they will lose more than they will gain, since they could easily fail with materializing. And this is what prompted me to compose a sufficient interpretation to the writings of the Ari, and now to the Holy *Zohar*. And I have completely removed that concern, for I have evidently explained and proven the spiritual meaning of everything, that it is abstract and devoid of any corporeal image, above space and above time, as the readers will see, to allow the whole of Israel to study *The Book of Zohar* and be warmed by its sacred Light.

Baal HaSulam, "Introduction to The Book of Zohar," Item 58

We can see that all the interpretations of *The Book of Zohar* before ours did not clarify as much as ten percent of the difficult places in *The Zohar*. And in the little they did clarify, their words are almost as abstruse as the words of *The Zohar* itself.

But in our generation we have been rewarded with the *Sulam* (Ladder) commentary, which is a complete interpretation of all the words of *The Zohar*. Moreover, not only does it not leave an unclear matter in the whole of *The Zohar* without interpreting it, but the clarifications are based on a straightforward analysis, which any intermediate student can understand. And since *The Zohar* appeared in our generation, it is a clear proof that we are already in the days of the Messiah, at the outset of that generation upon which it was said, "for the earth shall be full of the knowledge of the Lord."

Baal HaSulam, "A Speech for the Completion of The Zohar"

This is what I have troubled to do in this interpretation, to explain the ten *Sefirot* as the Godly sage the Ari had instructed us, in their spiritual purity, devoid of any tangible terms. Thus, any beginner may approach the wisdom without failing in any materialization and mistake. With the understanding of these ten *Sefirot*, one will also come to examine and know how to comprehend the other issues in this wisdom.

Baal HaSulam, *The Study of the Ten Sefirot*, Part 1, "Inner Reflection"

And who better than I knows that I am not at all worthy of being even a messenger and a scribe for disclosing such secrets, and much less to thoroughly understand them. And why has the Creator done so to me? It is only because the generation is worthy of it, as it is the last generation, which stands at the threshold of complete redemption. And for this reason, it is worthy of beginning to hear the voice of Messiah's *Shofar*, which is the revealing of the secrets, as has been explained.

Baal HaSulam, "Messiah's *Shofar* [horn]"

THE LANGUAGE OF KABBALAH

The Wisdom of Kabbalah Does Not Speak of Our Corporeal World

All the words of the Torah are sublime secrets.

> *The Book of Zohar* with the *Sulam* [Ladder] Commentary,
> *BeHaalotecha*, Item 58

The Torah is spirituality.

> Rabbi Nachman of Breslev, Collections of the Moharan, 1

The wisdom of Kabbalah mentions nothing of our corporeal world.

> Baal HaSulam, "The Freedom"

The Zohar speaks nothing of corporeal incidents, but of the upper worlds, where there is no sequence of times as it is in corporeality.

85

Spiritual time is elucidated by change of forms and degrees that are above time and place.

The Book of Zohar with the *Sulam* [Ladder] Commentary,
VaYetze, Item 139

The wisdom of Kabbalah speaks only from the root of *Assiya* in spirituality and upward.

Rabbi Nachman of Breslev, *Collections of the Moharan*, 225

The secrets of the Torah are clothed in allegories and riddles in the Torah because of the spreading of the Torah and its descent from the sublime degree to this corporeal world.

Ramak, *Know the God of Thy Father*, 14

Regarding the entry, *Adam Kadmon*, I was appalled to see that a corporeal form was depicted for the concept of *Adam Kadmon* of the Kabbalah, which is only a metaphysical concept, a Godly concept. God forbid that we should allow ourselves to materialize these sacred concepts, even as a way of studying.

Rav Raiah *Kook, Letters*, Vol 1, 162

Woe to that person who says that the Torah is meant to tell literal stories, and in uneducated words of Esau, Laban, etc., for if that were the case, even today we could turn words of an uneducated into a Torah, and even nicer ones than they. If the Torah is meant to show mundane matters, even world rulers have better things among them. Let, Let us follow them and make them into a Torah as well. Rather, all the words of the Torah are sublime secrets.

The Book of Zohar with the *Sulam* [Ladder] Commentary,
BeHaalotecha, Item 58

Such is the Torah. It has a body, which is the *Mitzvot* of the Torah, called "bodies of the Torah." This body clothes in dresses, which are stories of this world. The fools in the world see only that clothing, which is the story in the Torah, and know nothing more. They do not observe what exists underneath the clothing of the Torah.

The Book of Zohar with the *Sulam* [Ladder] Commentary,
BeHaalotecha, Item 62

This story in the Torah is the clothing of the Torah. Whoever thinks that that clothing is the actual Torah, and that there is nothing else within it, will be cursed and he will have no share in the next world. This is why David said, "Open my eyes, that I may behold wondrous things from Your law [Torah]," observing what is beneath the clothing of the Torah.

The Book of Zohar with the *Sulam* [Ladder] Commentary,
BeHaalotecha, Item 60

Woe to those wicked ones who say that the Torah is no more than a story, and regard only the clothing. Happy are the righteous who view the Torah appropriately. Wine lies only in the jug; likewise, the Torah lies only in that clothing. Hence, we should consider what exists beneath the clothing. Thus, all of those stories are the clothing.

The Book of Zohar with the *Sulam* [Ladder] Commentary,
BeHaalotecha, Item 64

There is a strict condition during the engagement in this wisdom – to not materialize the matters with imaginary and corporeal issues. This is because thus they breach, "Thou shall not make unto thee a graven image, nor any manner of likeness." In that event, one is rather harmed instead of receiving benefit.

Baal HaSulam, "Introduction to the Study of the Ten Sefirot," Item 156

The Law of Roots and Branches

So it is with the worlds, where each lower world is an imprint of the world Above it.

Baal HaSulam, "The Essence of the Wisdom of Kabbalah"

The whole of reality that we detect in the conduct of nature in this world is only because they are so extended and drawn out from laws and conducts in the Upper, Spiritual Worlds.

Baal HaSulam, "The Freedom"

Through the clothing of the Torah you enter its internality. There is nothing in the revealed Torah that was not caused by the concealed. It is like a seal imprinted in wax—there is no protrusion or depression in the imprint that does not exist in the seal.

Ramak, *Know the God of Thy Father*, 67

The *Mitzvot* in the Torah are no more than laws and conducts set in Higher Worlds, which are the roots of all of nature's conducts in this world of ours. The laws of the Torah always match the laws of nature in this world as two drops in a pond.

Baal HaSulam, "The Freedom"

Kabbalists have found that the form of the four worlds, named *Atzilut*, *Beria*, *Yetzira*, and *Assiya*, beginning with the first, highest world, called *Atzilut*, and ending in this corporeal, tangible world, called *Assiya*, is exactly the same in every item and event. This means that everything that eventuates and occurs in the first world is found unchanged in the next world, below it, too.

It is likewise in all the worlds that follow it, down to this tangible world. There is no difference between them, but only a different degree, perceived in the substance of the elements of reality in each world.

Baal HaSulam, "The Essence of the Wisdom of Kabbalah"

Each of the manifold still, vegetative, animate, and speaking in this world have their corresponding parts in the world Above it, without any difference in their form, but only in their substance. Thus, an animal or a rock in this world is a corporeal matter, and its corresponding animal or rock in the Higher World is a spiritual matter, occupying no place or time. However, their quality is the same.

And here we should certainly add the matter of relation between matter and form, which is naturally conditioned on the quality of form, too. Similarly, with the majority of the still, vegetative, animate, and speaking in the Upper World, you will find their similitude and likeness in the world Above the Upper. This continues through the first world, where all the elements are completed, as it is written, "And God saw every thing that He had made, and, behold, it was very good."

Baal HaSulam, "The Teaching of the Kabbalah and Its Essence"

The substance of the elements of reality in the first, Uppermost world, is purer than in all the ones below it. And the substance of the elements of reality in the second world is coarser than in that of the first world, but purer than all that is of a lower degree.

This continues similarly down to this world before us, whose substance of the elements in reality is coarser and darker than in all the worlds preceding it. However, the shapes and the elements of reality and all their occurrences come unchanged and equal in every world, both in quantity and quality.

They compared it to the conduct of a seal and its imprint: all the shapes in the seal are perfectly transferred in every detail and intricacy to the imprinted object.

Baal HaSulam, "The Essence of the Wisdom of Kabbalah"

Each lower world is an imprint of the world Above it. Hence, all the forms in the Higher World are meticulously copied, in both quantity and quality, to the lower world.

Thus, there is not an element of reality, or an occurrence of reality in a lower world, that you will not find its likeness in the world Above it, as identical as two drops in a pond. And they are called "Root and Branch." That means that the item in the lower world is deemed a branch of its pattern, found in the Higher World, being the root of the lower element, as this is where that item in the lower world was imprinted and made to be.

That was the intention of our sages when they said, "You haven't a blade of grass below that has not a fortune and a guard above that strike it and tells it, 'Grow'!" (Omissions of *The Zohar*, p 251a, *Beresheet Rabba*, Chapter 10). It follows that the root, called "fortune," compels it to grow and assume its attribute in quantity and quality, as with the seal and the imprint. This is the law of Root and Branch, which applies to every detail and occurrence of reality, in every single world, in relation to the world Above it.

Baal HaSulam, "The Essence of the Wisdom of Kabbalah"

There is nothing in the reality of the lower world that does not stem from its Superior World. As with the seal and the imprint, the root in the Upper World compels its branch in the lower one to reveal its entire form and feature, as our sages said, that the fortune in the world Above, related to the grass in the world below, strikes it, forcing it to complete its growth. Because of that, each and every branch in this world well defines its mold, situated in the Higher World.

Baal HaSulam, "The Essence of the Wisdom of Kabbalah"

The corporeal mount before us, called Mount Olives, also has relation of a borrowing in that name. This is the meaning of the words, "And his feet stood upon Mount Olives on that day..." Thus, it is clear that if one with attainment named this mountain so, he certainly understood the complete perception of that name. And if some nefarious person [named this mountain], surely... it so happened that he regarded its soil good for olives, or that he saw many olive trees growing on it, or something of the kind.

Baal HaSulam, *Ohr HaBahir [The Bright Light]*, Mount Olives

The Language of the Kabbalists Is a Language of Branches

The language of Kabbalists is a language in the full sense of the word: very precise, both concerning root and branch and concerning cause and consequence. It has a unique merit of being able to express subtle details in this language without any limits. Also, through it, it is possible to approach the desired matter directly, without the need to connect it with what precedes it or follows it.

Baal HaSulam, "The Teaching of the Kabbalah and Its Essence"

Kabbalists have found a set and annotated vocabulary, sufficient to create an excellent spoken language. It enables them to converse with one another of the dealings in the Spiritual Roots in the Upper Worlds by merely mentioning the lower, tangible branch in this world that is well defined to our corporeal senses. The listeners understand the Upper Root to which this corporeal branch points because it is related to it, being its imprint.

Baal HaSulam, "The Essence of the Wisdom of Kabbalah"

All the beings of the tangible creation and all their instances have become to them like well-defined words and names, indicating the High Spiritual Roots. Although there cannot be a verbal expression in their spiritual place, as it is above any imagination, they have earned the right to be expressed by utterance through their branches, arranged before our senses here in the tangible world.

Baal HaSulam, "The Essence of the Wisdom of Kabbalah"

All the words and utterances our lips pronounce cannot help us convey even a single word from the spiritual, Godly matters, above the imaginary time and space. Instead, there is a special language for these matters, being the Language of the Branches, indicating their relation to their Upper Roots.

However, this language, though extremely suitable for its task of delving into the studies of this wisdom, more than other languages, is only so if the listener is wise in his own right, meaning that he knows and understands the way the branches relate to their roots.

Baal HaSulam, "The Essence of the Wisdom of Kabbalah"

All those who attained the Light of the Creator through their work wanted all those succeeding them to enjoy what they had already discovered, as well. Therefore, they named each and every attainment so they would be able to understand their intentions and the attainments that they attained, and thus form a common language with each other.

Rabash, "Letter no. 19"

All the Languages Are Included in the Wisdom of Kabbalah

The internality of the wisdom of Kabbalah is none other than the internality of the Bible, the Talmud, and the legends. The only difference between them is in their explanations. This is similar to a wisdom that has been translated into four languages. Naturally, the essence of the wisdom has not changed at all by the change of language. All we need to think of is which translation is the most convenient for conveying the wisdom to the student.

Baal HaSulam, "The Teaching of the Kabbalah and Its Essence"

The names, appellations, and *Gematrias* belong entirely to the wisdom of Kabbalah. The reason they are found in the other languages, too [Bible, laws, and legends], is that all the languages are included in the wisdom of Kabbalah. This is so because these are all particular cases that the other languages must be assisted with.

But one should not think that these four languages, which serve to explain the wisdom of Godly revelation, evolved one at a time, over time. The truth is that all four appeared before the sages simultaneously. In truth, each consists of all the others. The language of Kabbalah exists in the Bible, such as the standing on the *Tzur* (rock), the thirteen attributes of mercy in the Torah and in *Micah*, and, to an extent, it is sensed in each and every verse. There are also the chariots in Isaiah and Ezekiel, and atop them all *The Song of Songs*, all of which is purely the language of Kabbalah. It is similar in laws and in legends, and all the more so with the matter of the unerasable holy names, which bear the same meaning in all the languages.

Baal HaSulam, "The Teaching of the Kabbalah and Its Essence"

The Concealed Torah and the Revealed Torah

Attainment of the Torah Begins with *Sod* [Secret] and Ends with *Peshat* [Literal]

Who would dare extract it from the heart of the masses and scrutinize their ways, when their attainment is incomplete in both parts of the Torah called *Peshat* (literal) and *Drush* (interpretation)? In their view, the order of the four parts of the Torah (PARDESS) begins with the *Peshat*, then the *Drush*, then *Remez* (insinuated), and in the end the *Sod* (Secret) is understood.

However, it is written in the Vilna Gaon prayer book that the attainment begins with the *Sod*. After the *Sod* part of the Torah is attained it is possible to attain the *Drush* part, and then the *Remez* part. When one is granted complete knowledge of these three parts of the Torah, one is awarded the attainment of the Peshat part of the Torah.

Baal HaSulam, "Introduction to the Book, Panim Meirot uMasbirot," Item 1

The concealed Torah implies that the Creator hides in the Torah, hence the name, "the Torah of the hidden." Conversely, it is called "revealed" because the Creator is revealed by the Torah.

Therefore, the Kabbalists said, and we also find it in the prayer book of the Vilna Gaon (GRA), that the order of attainment of the Torah begins with the concealed and ends with the revealed. This means that through the appropriate labor, where one first delves into the Torah of the hidden, he is thus granted the revealed Torah, the literal. Thus, one begins with the concealed, called *Sod* (secret), and when he is rewarded, he ends in the literal.

Baal HaSulam, "Introduction to The Study of the Ten Sefirot," Item 103

Great merit is required in order to understand the *Peshat* of the texts, since first we must attain the three internal parts of the Torah, which the *Peshat* robes, and the *Peshat* will not be parsed...

It is the opposite of the argument of the negligent in attaining the interior, who say to themselves: "We settle for attaining the *Peshat*. If we attain that, we will be content." Their words can be compared to one who wishes to step on the fourth step without first stepping on the first three steps.

Baal HaSulam, "Introduction to the Book, Panim Meirot uMasbirot," Item 1

Now you will understand the truth in the words of the Vilna *Gaon* in the prayer book, in the blessing for the Torah. He wrote that the Torah begins with *Sod* (secret), meaning the revealed Torah of *Assyia*, which is considered hidden, since the Creator is completely hidden there.

Then he moves on to the *Remez* (intimation), meaning that He is more revealed in the Torah of *Yetzira*. Finally, one attains the *Peshat* (literal), which is the Torah of *Atzilut*. It is called *Peshat*, for it is *Mufshat* (stripped) of all the clothes that conceal the Creator.

Baal HaSulam, "Introduction to The Study of the Ten Sefirot," Item 148

Studying the Concealed Torah Is Preferable to the Revealed Torah

It is impossible for the whole of Israel to come to that great purity except through the study of Kabbalah, which is the easiest way, adequate even for commoners. However, while engaging only in the revealed Torah, it is impossible to be rewarded through it, except for a chosen few and after great efforts, but not for the majority of the people.

Baal HaSulam, "Introduction to The Study of the Ten Sefirot," Item 36

It is easier to draw the light in the Torah while practicing and laboring in the wisdom of truth than in laboring in the literal Torah. The reason is very simple: the wisdom of the revealed is clothed in external, corporeal clothes, such as stealing, plundering, torts, etc. For this reason, it is difficult and heavy for any person to aim his mind and heart to the Creator while studying, so as to draw the Light in the Torah.

It is even more so for a person for whom the study in the Talmud itself is heavy and arduous. How can he remember the Creator during the study, since the scrutiny concerns corporeal matters, and cannot come in him simultaneously with the intention for the Creator?

Therefore, he advises him to practice the wisdom of Kabbalah, as this wisdom is entirely clothed in the names of the Creator. Then he will certainly be able to easily aim his mind and heart to the Creator during the study, even if he is the slowest learner. This is so because the study of the issues of the wisdom and the Creator are one and the same.

Baal HaSulam, "Introduction to The Study
of the Ten Sefirot," Item 22

Even though they do not succeed through the practice in the revealed Torah, since there is no Light in it, and it is dry due to the smallness of their minds, they could still succeed by engaging in the study of Kabbalah. This is because the Light in it is clothed in the clothing of the Creator – the Holy Names and the *Sefirot*. They could easily come to that form of *Lo Lishma*, which brings them to *Lishma*.

Baal HaSulam, "Introduction to The Study
of the Ten Sefirot," Item 35

Previously, the revealed Torah sufficed. But now, in the days of the Messiah, there is a need for the hidden Torah, as well. It is as we see with a burning candle: before it quenches, its flame grows much stronger and higher. Also, previously, the evil inclination was not so strong, and the revealed Torah was sufficient as a spice against it. But now, prior to the redemption, the evil inclination is intensifying and requires strengthening through the hidden, too.

Rav Simcha Bonim of Pshischa, *A Torah of Joy*, p 57

The Braita warns us (*Hulin* 24) to not wait longer than five years. Moreover, Rabbi Yosi says that only three years are quite sufficient to be granted the wisdom of the Torah.

If one does not see a good sign within that length of time, one should not fool himself with false hopes and deceit, but know that he will never see a good sign. Hence, one must immediately find himself a good tactic by which to succeed in achieving *Lishma* and to be granted the wisdom of the Torah...

This is the meaning of the Rav's words, that the surest and most successful tactic is the engagement in the wisdom of Kabbalah. One should leave one's hand entirely from engagement in the wisdom of the revealed Torah, since he has already tested his luck in it and did not succeed. And he should dedicate all his time to the wisdom of Kabbalah, where his success is certain.

Baal HaSulam, "Introduction to The Study of the Ten Sefirot," Item 23

If we examine his words they will clarify before us as pure heavenly stars. The text, "he is better off leaving his hand off it, once he has tested his luck in this [revealed] wisdom," does not refer to luck of wit and erudition. Rather, it is as we have explained above in the explanation, "I have created the evil inclination; I have created for it the spice of Torah."

It means that one has delved and exerted in the revealed Torah, and still the evil inclination is in power and has not melted at all. This is because he is still not saved from thoughts of transgression ... Hence, he advises him to leave his hands off it and engage in the wisdom of truth.

Baal HaSulam, "Introduction to The Study of the Ten Sefirot," Item 22

I answered a scholar who asked about the writings of the students of the Ari, that the study of *The Zohar* is a great correction with which to illuminate the soul and to sanctify it. The Ari gave this correction to one who was repenting to study five pages of *The Zohar* each day, even though he did not know what it said, for that reading illuminates the soul and corrects it. It seems that the study of *The Zohar* specifically has that power, more than the study of Mishnah, Talmud and Bible, and it is a wonder, the way its power is greater than the entire

Torah, whether it is the Bible or the Mishnah, etc., those are his words.

And I told him that undoubtedly, any study of the Torah is exalted and uplifting, particularly if it is truly *Lishma* [for Her name]. Surely, it builds its ascensions in heaven and corrects the worlds and unites the beloved. Still, the greatness of the study of *The Zohar* is that the Bible, the Mishnah, and the Talmud are excessively clothed, and the concealed is completely indiscernible in them. *The Zohar*, however, speaks explicitly of the secrets of Torah, and even the most illiterate reader will realize that its words stem from the depths of the secrets of Torah. Thus, as the secrets of the Torah are revealed and unclothed, they illuminate and radiate the soul.

The Chida, *HaGedolim* [*The Great Ones*], Set of Books, 2

WHO IS SUITABLE
FOR STUDYING KABBALAH

Concerning the Obligation of Each Person to Study the Wisdom of Kabbalah

The study of the wisdom of Kabbalah is an absolute must for any person from Israel.

Baal HaSulam, "Introduction to, The Mouth of a Sage"

The Creator feels no contentment in His world except when people engage in this wisdom. Moreover, man was created only to study the wisdom of Kabbalah.

Rav Chaim Vital, "Preface to the Gate to Introductions"

The direction of revealing the secrets of the Torah is the ideal goal in life and reality.

Rav Raiah Kook, *The Lights of Sanctity*, 1, 142

It is of utter necessity for anyone from Israel, whoever he may be, to engage in the internality of the Torah and in its secrets. Without it, the intention of Creation will not be completed in him.

Baal HaSulam, "Introduction to The Mouth of a Sage"

The redemption of Israel and the rise of Israel depend on the study of *The Zohar* and the internality of the Torah.

Baal HaSulam, "Introduction to The Book of Zohar," Item 69

Redemption will come only by studying Torah, and redemption depends on the study of Kabbalah.

The Vilna Gaon (GRA),
Even Shlemah (*A Perfect and Just Weight*), Chapter 11, Item 3

All the more so, with all of our heart, spirit and might, we should pursue the wisdom of faith, which is the wisdom of the path of Kabbalah, the path of truth.

The Baal Shem Tov,
Me'irot Eynayim [*Illuminating the Eyes*] Portion *Re'eh* [See]

In proximity to the generations approximately a thousand years after the ruin, the Light of *The Zohar* appeared, to protect the generations. If we are rewarded with engaging in the secrets of Torah and do it properly, by that the salvation of Israel will spread.

The Chida, *HaGedolim* [*The System of the Great Ones*], 1, 219

The secrets of Torah bring the redemption; they bring Israel back to its land.

Rav Raiah Kook, *Orot* [*Lights*], 95

Precisely at a time of great peril and crisis we should take the best of cures.

The Rav Raiah Kook, *Igrot* [*Letters*], Vol. 2, pp 123, 125

The Creator commands us to know His Providence, and indeed we want to study what this Providence will teach us. What this Providence teaches us is none other than the wisdom of truth, which is the study of His Divinity. Accordingly, we see the obligation to study the wisdom of the truth beyond any doubt.

Ramchal, *The Gates of Ramchal*, "The Dispute"

The young, or those who find themselves heavy and of little desire for the Inner Light, must, at the very least, make it a rule to dedicate one or two hours a day to the wisdom of truth. In time, their minds will broaden.

Rav Raiah Kook, *Letters of the Raiah*, 1, 82

There is no doubt that out all the teachings in the world, none is more important than pursuing the secrets of Torah, for they concern Divinity, since the intention in His giving of the Torah to Israel was to know the Creator and to serve Him.

Rav Moshe Cordovero (Ramak), *Know the God of Thy Father*, 5

It is well-known how that it is an immense obligation for one to study the wisdom of truth, which is the wisdom of Kabbalah and the secrets of the Torah, as explained in ancient books.

Rabbi Baruch Ben Abraham of Kosov,
Amud Ha'Avoda [Pillar of the Work] p1

If my people heeded me in this generation, when heresy prevails, they would delve in the study of *The Book of Zohar* and the *Tikkunim* [Corrections], contemplating them with nine-year-old infants. Thus, the fear of sin would precede his wisdom and he would persist.

Rav Yitzhak Yehuda Yehiel of Komarno,
Notzer Hesed [*Keeping Mercy*], Chapter 4, Teaching 20

The resulting rule is that one must know the Creator, and one who has not seen this wisdom has never seen lights in his life, and the fool walks in darkness.

Rabbi Chaim Vital, *Otzrot HaChaim* [*The Treasures of Life*] p 18

The prohibition from Above to refrain from open study of the wisdom of truth was for a limited period, until the end of 1490. Thereafter is considered the last generation, in which the prohibition was lifted and permission has been granted to engage in *The Book of Zohar*. And since the year 1540, it has been a great *Mitzva* (precept) for the masses to study, old and young. And since the Messiah is bound to come as a result, and for no other reason, it is inappropriate to be negligent.

Abraham Ben Mordechai Azulai, Introduction to the book, *Ohr HaChama (Light of the Sun)* 81

It is known from books and from authors that the study of the wisdom of Kabbalah is an absolute must for any person from Israel. And if one studies the whole Torah and knows the Mishnah and the Gemarah by heart, and if one is also filled with virtues and good deeds more than all his contemporaries, but has not learned the wisdom of Kabbalah, he must reincarnate into this world to study the secrets of Torah and wisdom of truth. This is brought in several places in the writing of our sages.

Baal HaSulam, "Introduction to The Mouth of a Sage"

Why then, did the Kabbalists obligate each person to study the wisdom of Kabbalah? Indeed, there is a great thing in it, worthy of being publicized: There is a wonderful, invaluable remedy to those who engage in the wisdom of Kabbalah. Although they do not understand what they are learning, through the yearning and the great desire to understand what they are learning, they awaken upon themselves the Lights that surround their souls.

This means that every person from Israel is guaranteed to finally attain all the wonderful attainments that the Creator had contemplated in the Thought of Creation to delight every creature. And one who has not been awarded in this life will be granted in the next life, etc., until one is awarded completing His Thought, which He had planned for him.

Baal HaSulam, "Introduction to The Study of the Ten Sefirot," Item 155

Before us is an obligation to expand and establish the engagement in the inner side of the Torah, in all its spiritual issues, which, in its broader sense, includes the broad wisdom of Israel, whose apex is the knowledge of God in truth, according to the depth of the secrets of Torah. These days, it requires elucidation, scrutiny, and explanation, to make it ever clearer and ever more expansive among our entire nation.

Rav Raiah Kook,
Otzrot HaRaiah [Treasures of the Raiah], 2, 317

The Torah was given to learn and to teach so that all will know the thought of the Creator, from small to great. We also found in many books by Kabbalist, cautions regarding the study of this wisdom—that everyone must study it.

Rabbi Yitzhak Ben Tzvi Ashkenazi,
Taharat HaKodesh [The Purity of Sanctity], 147

At the time of the Messiah, evil, impudence, and vice will increase, led by the heads of the mixed multitude. Then the Hidden Light will appear out of Heaven—*The Book of Zohar* and the *Tikkunim [Corrections]*, followed by the writings of our teacher, the Ari. And that study will root out the evil in his soul, he will be rewarded with adhering to the Upper Light, and will be rewarded with all the virtues in the world.

Rav Yitzhak Yehuda Yehiel Safrin of Komarno, *Heichal HaBerachah* [*The Hall of Blessing*], *Devarim (Deuteronomy)*, 208

It is impossible for the whole of Israel to come to that great purity except through the study of Kabbalah, which is the easiest way, adequate even for commoners.

However, while engaging only in the revealed Torah, it is impossible to be rewarded through it, except for a chosen few and after great efforts, but not for the majority of the people.

Baal HaSulam, "Introduction to The Study of the Ten Sefirot" Item 36

Let us hope that all our brothers in the house of Israel will study of *The Book of Zohar* together, rich and poor, young and old.

And how good and how pleasant if they try to establish friendships for the study of *The Zohar*. Particularly now, when the sparks of redemption have begun to blossom, we should exert in this sacred study, which can bring the Messiah.

Introduction of the Rabbis to *The Zohar*, Jerba Printing

As long as the inner soul is deprived of its natural nourishment, it gradually depletes, withers and degenerates. Therefore ... we should bring the Light inside, and assertively determine consistent and organized study, as an unbreakable law ... of the spiritual study ... until one reaches the boundary of the Godly wisdom at the source of Israel—the wisdom of truth and the Kabbalah and all its details.

Rav Raiah Kook, *Treasures of the Raiah*, 2, 319

Since the whole of the wisdom of Kabbalah speaks of the revelation of the Creator, naturally, there is none more successful teaching for its task. This is what the Kabbalists aimed for—to arrange it so it is suitable for studying.

And so they studied in it until the time of concealment (it was agreed to conceal it for a certain reason). However, this was only for a certain time, and not forever, as it is written in *The Zohar*, "This wisdom is destined to be revealed at the end of days, and even to children."

Baal HaSulam, "The Teaching of the Kabbalah and Its Essence"

Many fools escape from studying the secrets of the Ari and *The Book of Zohar*, which are our lives. If my people heeded me in the time of the Messiah, when evil and heresy increase, they would delve in the study of *The Book of Zohar* and the *Tikkunim* [corrections] and the writings of the Ari, and they would revoke all the harsh sentences and would extend abundance and Light.

Rav Yitzhak Yehuda Yehiel of Komarno,
Notzer Hesed (*Keeping Mercy*), Chapter 4, Teaching 20

Now it is upon us, relics, to correct that dreadful wrong. Each of us remainders should take upon himself, heart and soul, to henceforth intensify the internality of the Torah, and give it its rightful place, according to its merit over the externality of the Torah.

Baal HaSulam, "Introduction to The Book of Zohar," Item 71

Not only are these secrets not forbidden to disclose, on the contrary, it is a great *Mitzva* (very good deed) to disclose them (as written in *Pesachim* 119). And one who knows how to disclose and discloses them, his reward is plentiful. This is because on disclosing these Lights to many, particularly to the many, depends the coming of Messiah soon in our days Amen.

Baal HaSulam, "Introduction to The Study of the Ten Sefirot," Item 30

I have agreed to disclose all the secrets of the world, since it is time to do unto the Creator, as it is required at this time. Greater and better than I have suffered nationwide slander for such matters, as their pure spirit pressured them for the sake of the correcting the generation, to speak new words and to reveal the concealed, to which the intellect of the masses was not accustomed.

Rav Raiah Kook, Letters the Raiah 2, 34

They have no scientific solution as to how a spiritual object can have any contact with physical atoms to bring them into any kind of motion. All their wisdom and delving did not help them find a bridge on which to cross that wide and deep crevice that spreads between the spiritual entity and the corporeal atom. Thus, science has gained nothing from all these metaphysical methods.

... To move a step forward in a scientific manner here, all we need is the wisdom of Kabbalah. This is because all the teachings in the world are included in the wisdom of Kabbalah.

Baal HaSulam, "The Freedom"

Understanding the meaning of the word, "spirituality," has nothing to do with philosophy. This is because how can they discuss something that they have never seen or felt? What do their rudiments stand on? If there is any definition that can tell spiritual from corporeal, it belongs only to those who have attained a spiritual thing and felt it. These are the genuine Kabbalists; thus, it is the wisdom of Kabbalah that we need.

Baal HaSulam, "The Wisdom of Kabbalah and Philosophy"

Studying *The Zohar* at this time is much needed to save and to protect us from all evil, since the disclosure of this wisdom now, in flawed generations, is to be a shield for us to wholeheartedly cling to our Father in Heaven. Previous generations were men of action and pious, and the good deeds saved them from the accusers. Now we are remote from the Higher Root like the yeast in the barrel. Who will protect us if not our study of this wisdom?

The Sage Yaakov Tzemach in his introduction to *The Tree of Life*

Turning the hearts and occupying the minds with noble thoughts, whose origin is the secrets of the Torah.

The Rav Raiah Kook, *Mist of Purity*, p 65

We should exalt the entire Torah in its spiritual interpretations.

Rav Raiah Kook, *Letters 2*

Imagine, for example, that some historic book were to be found today that depicts the last generations ten thousand years from now, for as you and we feel, the lessons of the torments and slaughtering will certainly suffice to reform them into good comportments.

And these people, before them are good comportments that serve them to provide sustenance and complacency, or at least to guarantee a daily life of peace and quiet. Undoubtedly, if some sage were to provide us with this book of the wisdom of statesmanship and the conducts of the individual, our leaders would seek out every counsel to arrange life accordingly, and there would "No outcry in our streets." Corruption and the terrible slayings would cease, and everything would come peacefully to its place.

Now, distinguished readers, this book lies here before you in a closet. It states explicitly all the wisdom of statesmanship and the behavior of private and public life that will exist at the end of days. It is the books of Kabbalah, where the corrected worlds are set. They emerged perfect, as it says, perfection emerges first from the Creator, then we correct it and come to complete and lasting perfection in the Upper World.

It stems from the Creator as "the end of a matter is in the first thought." ... Open these books and you will find all the good comportment that will appear and the end of days, and from them, you will find the good lesson by which to arrange mundane matters today, as well. We can examine past history and by that correct the future history.

Baal HaSulam, *Writings of the Last Generation*

Rabbi Shem-Tov has already written in *The Book of the Faiths* that only by the wisdom of Kabbalah would Judah and Israel be saved forever, for only this is the Godly wisdom delivered to the sages of Israel in ancient times and ancient years. Through it, the glory of the Creator and the glory of His law will be revealed.

Rabbi Shabtai Ben-Yaakov Yitzhak Lifshitz, *Segulat Yisrael [The Remedy of Israel]* System no. 7, Item 5

When the days of the Messiah draw near, even infants in the world will find the secrets of the wisdom, knowing in them the end and the calculations of redemption. At the same time, it will be revealed to all.

The Book of Zohar with the *Sulam* [Ladder] Commentary, *VaYera*, Item 460

But most importantly, know, my brother, that this study has been revealed so brightly and expansively at this time primarily because the evil is greatly increasing and the assembly of Israel is falling. Through this study, the soul is purified. Indeed, while studying the secrets, and particularly *The Book of Zohar* and the *Tikkunim* [corrections], the soul illuminates.

Rabbi Yitzchak Isaac Yehuda Yechiel Safrin of Komarno, *The Path of your Commandments*, Introduction, "The Path of Unification," 1, Item 4

The whole part of the revealed Torah is but a preparation to become worthy and merit attaining the concealed part. It is the concealed part that is the very wholeness and the purpose for which man is created.

Hence, clearly, if a part of the concealed part is missing, although one may keep the Torah and observe its commandments in the revealed part, he will still have to reincarnate to this world and receive what he should receive, namely the concealed part, by way of 613 deposits. Only in that is the soul completed, the way the Creator had predetermined for it.

Baal HaSulam, "Introduction to The Mouth of a Sage"

The Opposition to the Study of the Wisdom of Kabbalah

Now you can understand the aridity and the darkness that have befallen us in this generation, such as we have never seen before. It is because even the worshipers of the Creator have abandoned the engagement in the secrets of the Torah.

Baal HaSulam, "Introduction to The Book of Zohar," Item 57

All the great Kabbalists unanimously cry out like cranes that as long as we deny the Torah of its secrets and do not engage in its secrets, we are destroying the world.

The Rav Raiah Kook, *Igrot (Letters)*, Vol. 2, p 231

I see that the primary reason for the lack of success in everything being done to strengthen Judaism and Israel's status everywhere, is that the Divine Light has been neglected, completely abandoned by heart and mind. Everyone is now turning to correct simple ultra-orthodoxy alone, as if the world could be revived in a body with no soul.

Rav Raiah Kook, Letters 1, 160-161

Many fools escape from studying the secrets of the Ari and *The Book of Zohar*, which are our lives. If my people heeded me in the time of the Messiah, when evil and heresy increase, they would delve in the study of *The Book of Zohar* and the *Tikkunim* [corrections] and the writings of the Ari, and they would revoke all the harsh sentences and would extend abundance and Light.

Rav Yitzhak Yehuda Yehiel of Komarno,
Notzer Hesed (Keeping Mercy), Chapter 4, Teaching 20

Woe unto them that make the spirit of Messiah leave and depart from the world, and cannot return to the world. They are the ones that make the Torah dry, without any moisture of comprehension and reason. They confine themselves to the practical part of the Torah, and do not wish to try to understand the wisdom of Kabbalah, to know and to understand the secrets of the Torah and the flavors of Mitzva. Woe unto them, for with these actions they bring about the existence of poverty, ruin, and robbery, looting, killing, and destructions in the world.

Baal HaSulam, "Introduction to The Book of Zohar," Item 70

This is the reason why Rabbi Shimon Bar-Yochai so cried over it, and called upon those who engage in the literal Torah that they are asleep, for they do not open their eyes to see the love that the Creator loves them, as though they were, God forbid, ungrateful to Him. Moreover, they do not see and do not know the path of holiness and the Dvekut (adhesion) with Him at all.

Rav Moshe Chaim Luzzato (Ramchal), Shaarey Ramchal [Gates of the Ramchal], "The Debate," p 97

As long as orthodoxy insists on saying, "No! Only Gemarah and Mishnah, no legends, no ethics, no Kabbalah, and no research," it dwindles itself. All the means it uses to protect itself, without taking the true potion of life, the Light of the Torah in its internals, beyond the tangible and obvious—the revealed in the Torah and *Mitzvot*—are utterly incapable of leading to its goal in all the generations, and especially in our generation, unless accompanied by expanding the many spiritual roots.

The Rav Raiah Kook, *Igrot (Letters)*, Vol. 2, 232-233

Woe unto people from the affront of the Torah. For undoubtedly, when they engage only in the literal and in its stories, it wears its widow-garments, and covered with a bag. And all the nations shall say unto Israel: "What is thy Beloved more than another beloved? Why is your law more than our law? After all, your law, too, is stories of the mundane." There is no greater affront to the Torah than that.

Hence, woe unto the people from the affront of the Torah. They do not engage in the wisdom of Kabbalah, which honors the Torah, for they prolong the exile and all the afflictions that are about to come to the world.

Rav Chaim Vital, *The Writings of the Ari*, *The Tree of Life*,
Part One, "Rav Chaim Vital's Introduction," 11-12

It is well-known how that it is an immense obligation for one to study the wisdom of truth, which is the wisdom of Kabbalah and the secrets of the Torah, as explained in ancient books. ...And I wonder about the people of our generation, for the humble ones among them veer off from studying the wisdom of truth.

Rabbi Baruch Ben Abraham of Kosov,
Amud Ha'Avoda [*Pillar of the Work*], p1

They are the ones who make the Torah dry, for they do not wish to delve in the wisdom of Kabbalah. Woe unto them, for thus they cause wretchedness, ruin, looting, killing, and destruction to the world.

The Book of Zohar,
Tikkuney Zohar [The Zohar Corrections], Tikkun no. 30

Many thought that too much engagement in the secret is not good, since the practical Torah would be forgotten from Israel, the forbidden, the permitted, the non-kosher, and the kosher. And what shall become of this Torah had we all delved in the secrets of the Torah? ...Yet, those who despise it are not servants of the Creator whatsoever.

Rav Moshe Cordovero (Ramak),
Know the God of Thy Father, 132

Without knowing the wisdom of Kabbalah, one is like a beast, carrying out the precept with no purpose, only learning the precepts of man. This is similar to hay-eating beasts, without the taste of human food. And even if one is an important businessperson, occupied with many negotiations, he is not exempted from engaging in this wisdom.

Rabbi Tzvi Hirsh Eichenstein of Ziditshov, *Sur Me'ra Ve'aseh Tov [Depart from Evil and Do Good]*

All who refrain from studying Kabbalah is rejected from among the righteous, and loses his world, and is not rewarded with seeing the Light of Life's King's countenance.

Rav Yosef Eliezer Rosenfeld, *Havvot Yair [Villages of Yair]*, p 210

But if, God forbid, it is to the contrary, and a person from Israel degrades the virtue of the internality of the Torah and its secrets, which deals with the conduct of our souls and their degrees, and the perception and the tastes of the *Mitzvot* with regard to the advantage of the externality of the Torah, which deals only with the practical part? Also, even if one does occasionally engage in the internality of the Torah, and dedicates a little of one's time to it, when it is neither night nor day, as though it were redundant, by that one dishonors and degrades the internality of the world, which are the Children of Israel, and enhances the externality of the world—meaning the Nations of the World—over them. They will humiliate and disgrace the Children of Israel, and regard Israel as superfluous, as though the world has no need for them, God forbid.

Baal HaSulam, "Introduction to The Book of Zohar," Item 69

This is the answer to the wiseacre fools, with vain wisdom, who speak against those who engage in the wisdom of Kabbalah and say about them that they hear the voice of words, yet see no image. Woe unto them and to their misfortune for their foolishness and wantonness, for they will not profit from it; they only move God's people from rising unto His Holy Mountain.

Rav Shimon Ben Lavi, *Ketem Paz* [*Fine Gold*],
Good and Evil Are Contained in Man

Engaging in the wisdom of the Mishnah and the Babylonian Talmud without allotting a portion to the secrets and hidden wisdom of the Torah is similar to a body sitting in the dark, devoid of a man's soul, the Creator's candle that glows within. Thus, the body is dry, not inhaling from the source of life. This is the meaning of what he said above, "For they are the ones who are making the Torah dry and do not wish to exert in the wisdom of Kabbalah."

Rav Chaim Vital, "Introduction of Rav Chaim Vital to The Gate of the Introductions"

The crown of the Torah is the wisdom of Kabbalah, from which the majority of the world retires, saying that you should observe what is permitted and that you have no dealings in the hidden. You, if you are fit for this teaching, reach out your hand, hold it, and do not move from it. This is because one who did not taste the flavor of this wisdom, has never seen Lights in his life, and he is walking in the dark. And woe unto the people from the affront of this Torah.

Rabbi Pinchas Eliahu Ben-Meir, *Sefer HaBrit* [*The Book of the Covenant*], Part 2, Article 12, Chapter 5

I have seen in many books of Kabbalists, the magnitude of the tremendous and bitter punishment upon whoever avoided the study of wisdom of Kabbalah, along with the enhancement of the reward and the pleasure in the next world for whoever studies It.

Rabbi Baruch Ben Abraham of Kosov,
Amud Ha'Avoda [Pillar of the Work]

One who did not engage in the wisdom of truth, who did not want to learn it when his soul wanted to rise to the Garden of Eden, is rejected from there with disgrace.

Rabbi Pinchas Eliahu Ben-Meir, *Sefer HaBrit*
[*The Book of the Covenant*], Part 2, Article 12, Chapter 5

Engaging in Kabbalah Requires No Preliminary Excellence

From the words of the Gemarah: "A disciple who has not seen a good sign in his study after five years will also not see it." Why did he not see a good sign in his study? Certainly, it is only due to the absence of the intention of the heart, and not because of any lack of aptitude, as the wisdom of Torah requires no aptitude. Instead, as it is written in the above study: "The Creator said unto Israel, 'Regard, the whole wisdom and the whole Torah is easy: any one who fears Me and observes the words of the Torah, the whole wisdom and the whole Torah are in his heart.'"

Baal HaSulam, "Introduction to The Study of the Ten Sefirot," 23

If one is made ungifted, how can he be a wise disciple? His brain is too small to understand the words of Torah. Midrash Rabba says about that (portion, "And This Is the Blessing), "The Creator said unto Israel, 'The whole of the wisdom and the whole of the Torah are easy. Anyone who fears Me and practices the words of Torah, the whole of the wisdom and the whole of Torah are in his heart.'"

He explained about it in the "Introduction to The Study of the Ten Sefirot": "Thus, no prior aptitude is required here. Rather, by the fear of the Creator alone is one rewarded with the whole of the wisdom of the Torah. This is the meaning of, 'Everything is in the hands of the Creator except for the fear of the Creator.' This means that only the fear of the Creator requires choice, and the rest is given by the Creator."

Rabash, *Steps of the Ladder*, "The Ungifted"

During the practice of Torah, every person must labor in it, and set his mind and heart to find "the light of the king's countenance" in it, that is, the attainment of open Providence, called "light of countenance." And any person is fit for it, as it is written, "those that seek Me shall find Me," and as it is written, "I labored and did not find, do not believe." Thus, one needs nothing in this matter except the labor alone.

Baal HaSulam, "Introduction to The Study of the Ten Sefirot", Item 97

The purpose of creation is not necessarily for a select group. Rather, the purpose of creation belongs to all creations without exception. It is not necessarily the strong and skillful, or the brave people who can overcome. Rather, it belongs to all the creatures. (Examine the "Introduction to The Study of the Ten Sefirot," Item 21, where it quotes *Midrash Rabba*, Portion, "This is the Blessing": "The Creator said unto Israel: 'Regard, the whole wisdom and the whole of Torah are easy: Anyone who fears Me and does the words of Torah, the entire wisdom and the whole of the Torah are in his heart.'")

Rabash, *Rabash—the Social Writings*, "Love of Friends – 2"

Since the secrets of Torah come from a superior source—from the great concealment of the internality of the soul, a part of the Creator Above—they can enter all the hearts, even those hearts that have not reached the extent of expanded knowledge for acquiring a broad and deep science. And when they use that gift of theirs—the inclination toward the secrets of the Upper One, along with the acceptance of their scientific weakness, which fills them with humility, they bring a blessing to the world and reveal, with their pure desire, a great Light of the sages' knowledge.

Rav Raiah Kook, *Orot HaTorah* [*Lights of the Torah*] 10, 5

THE MEANING OF ISRAEL AND THE NATIONS OF THE WORLD

Yasher-El [Straight to the Creator]

Israel is he who strains himself to return to his root.

Baal HaSulam, *A Sage's Fruit, Letters*, Letter no. 17

One who wishes to go by the path of the Creator is called *Yashar-El*, which is considered *Yashar* [straight] *LaEl* [to God], meaning that he wants everything he does to rise straight to the Creator, and does not wish to have any other aim.

Rabash, *Rungs of the Ladder*,
"One who Strengthens One's Heart"

The word *Yashar-El* [Israel[is the letters of *Li Rosh* [I have a head (mind)], meaning that he believes he has a mind of *Kedusha* [Sanctity].

Baal HaSulam, *Shamati* [*I Heard*], 143, "Only Good to Israel"

Why Was the Torah Given to Israel?

Israel is the Creator's virtue, as it is said, "To be a virtuous nation unto Him."

Midrash Tana'im, Devarim [Deuteronomy], Chapter 14

Why was the Torah given to the Israeli nation without the participation of all the nations of the world?" The truth is that the purpose of creation applies to the entire human race, none absent. However, because of the lowness of the nature of creation and its power over people, it was impossible for people to be able to understand, determine and agree to rise above it. They did not demonstrate the desire to relinquish self-love and come to equivalence of form, which is adhesion with His attributes, as our sages said, "As He is merciful, so you be merciful."

Thus, because of their ancestral merit Israel succeeded, and over 400 years they developed and became qualified and sentenced themselves to a scale of merit. Each and every member of the nation agreed to love his fellow man.

Being a small and single nation among seventy great nations, when there are a hundred gentiles or more for every one of Israel, when they had taken upon themselves to love their fellow person, the Torah was then given specifically to qualify the Israeli nation.

Baal HaSulam, "The Love of the Creator and the Love of Others"

Rabbi Elazar, son of Rashbi (Rabbi Shimon Bar-Yochai), clarifies this concept of *Arvut* even further. It is not enough for him that all of Israel be responsible for one another, but the whole world is included in that *Arvut*. Indeed, there is no dispute here, for everyone admits that to begin with, it is enough to start with one nation for the observance of the Torah for the beginning of the correction of the world. It was impossible to begin with all the nations at once, as they said that the Creator went with the Torah to every nation and tongue, and they did not want to receive it. In other words, they were immersed in the filth of self-love up to their necks, some with adultery, some with robbery and murder and so on, until it was impossible to conceive, in those days, to even ask if they agreed to retire from self-love.

Therefore, the Creator did not find a nation or a tongue qualified to receive the Torah, except for the children of Abraham, Isaac, and Jacob, whose ancestral merit reflected upon them, as our sages said, "The Patriarchs observed the whole Torah even before it was given." This means that because of the exaltedness of their souls, they had the ability to attain all the ways of the Creator with respect to the spirituality of the Torah, which stems from their *Dvekut*, without first needing the ladder of the practical part of the Torah, which they had no possibility of observing at all.

Undoubtedly, both the physical purity and the mental exaltedness of our Holy Fathers greatly influenced their sons and their sons' sons, and their righteousness reflected upon that generation, whose members all assumed that sublime work, and each and every one stated clearly, "We shall do and we shall hear." Because of that, we were chosen, out of necessity, to be a chosen people from among all the nations. Hence, only the members of the Israeli nation were admitted into the required *Arvut*, and not the nations of the world at all, because they did not participate in it. And this is the plain reality.

Baal HaSulam, "The *Arvut* [mutual guarantee]," Item 19

It is written, "Ye shall be Mine own treasure from among all peoples." This means that you will be My treasure, and sparks of purification

147

and cleansing of the body shall pass through you onto all the peoples and the nations of the world, for the nations of the world are not yet ready for it. And at any rate, I need one nation to start with now, so it will be as a remedy for all the nations.

Baal HaSulam, "The *Arvut* [mutual guarantee]," Item 28

Judaism must present something new to the nations. That is what they expect from the return of Israel to the land! It is not in other teachings, for in that we never innovated; we were always their disciples. Rather, it is the wisdom of religion, justice and peace. In this, most nations are our disciples, and this wisdom is attributed to us alone.

Baal HaSulam, "The Solution"

The Assembly of Israel is the essence of the entire reality, and in this world, this essence is poured out in the actual Israeli nation, in its corporeality and spirituality, in its genealogy and its faith. The Israeli history is the essence of the ideal of the general history, and there is no movement in the world, in all the nations, whose similitude is not found in Israel. Its faith is the finest essence and the source that imparts the good and the idealism unto all the faiths. Thus, it is the force that questions all the terms of faith until it leads them to the degree of a clear language, for all to call the name of the Creator, "And your God is the Holy One of Israel, who is called the God of all the earth."

Rav Raiah Kook, *Orot [Lights]* 138

All of Israel Are Responsible for One Another

For all of Israel are responsible for one another.

Sanhedrin p 27b; *Shavuot* p 39a

"And Israel camped there, opposite from the mountain" (Exodus, 19). Our sages interpreted—as one man in one heart.

Baal HaSulam, "The meaning of Conception and Birth"

Israel are responsible for one another, meaning that the whole of Israel are one discernment.

Rabash, *Steps of the Ladder*, "Bride and Groom"

Through the force of *Arvut* [mutual guarantee], one corrects for another, and everything is corrected.

Ramchal, *Drushei*, 24 *Kishutei Callah* [Adornments of the Bride]

It is presented in *Midrash Tanchuma*, "Israel will not be redeemed until they are all one society, as it is said, 'In those days and at that time, says the Lord, the children of Israel shall come, they and the sons of Judah together.' Thus, when they are united, they receive the face of Divinity."

I presented the words of the Midrash so that you don't think that the issue of a group, which is love of friends, relates to Hassidism [a branch of Judaism]. Rather, it is the teaching of our sages, who saw how necessary was the unity of hearts into a single group for the reception of the face of Divinity.

Rabash, *Rabash—the Social Writings*, "Letter no. 34"

This is to speak of the *Arvut* [Mutual Guarantee], when all of Israel became responsible for one another. Because the Torah was not given to them before each and every one from Israel was asked if he agreed to take upon himself the *Mitzva* [precept] of loving others in the full measure, expressed in the words: "Love thy friend as thyself." This means that each and every one in Israel would take it upon himself to care and work for each member of the nation, and to satisfy all their every needs, no less than the measure imprinted in him to care for his own needs.

And once the whole nation unanimously agreed and said, "We shall do and we shall hear," each member of Israel became responsible that nothing shall be missing from any other member of the nation. Only then did they become worthy of receiving the Torah, and not before.

Baal HaSulam, "The *Arvut* [mutual guarantee]"

When one feels that one's soul exists in the whole of Israel, in each and every one of them... At that time, he is complete, flawless, and the soul truly shines on him in its fullest power, as it appeared in *Adam ha Rishon*.

Baal HaSulam, "600,000 Souls"

"There is a certain people scattered abroad and dispersed among the peoples."

Haman said that in his view, we will succeed in destroying the Jews because they are separated from one another; hence, our force against them will certainly prevail, as it causes separation between man and God. And the Creator will not help them anyway, since they are separated from Him. This is why Mordecai went to correct that flaw, as it is explained in the verse, "the Jews gathered," etc., "to gather themselves together, and to stand for their life." This means that they had saved themselves by uniting.

Baal HaSulam, *Shamati* [*I Heard*], 144,
"There is a Certain People"

"You are all beautiful, my wife." "The whole of the soul shall praise the Lord." The perfection of Divinity is in the soul of the Messiah King, who is an only daughter. However, to be complete, all the other souls must bond within her, and they all become one within Her, and then Divinity shines with great correction, for she is a bride. And then, "You are all beautiful, my wife, and there is no blemish" that remains, for through the force of the *Arvut*, one corrects for another, and everything is corrected.

Ramchal, *Drushei*, 24, *Kishutei Callah* [Adornments of the Bride]

Israel's Role Toward the World

Israel bring Light to the world.

Midrash Rabba, Song of Songs, Portion no. 4

A nation that any good that comes to the world, comes by its merit.

Beresheet Rabba, Portion no. 66

When the Children of Israel are complemented with the complete knowledge, the
fountains of intelligence and knowledge shall
flow beyond the boundaries of Israel and water all the nations of the world.

Baal HaSulam, "Introduction to the Book
Panim Meirot uMasbirot," Item 4

It is incumbent upon the Israeli nation to
qualify themselves and the rest of the people
in the world through engagement in Torah
and *Mitzvot Lishma* [for Her name], until
they evolve into assuming this sublime work
of love of others, which is the ladder to the
purpose of Creation, being *Dvekut* [adhesion]
with Him.

Baal HaSulam, "The *Arvut* [Mutual Guarantee]," Item 20

The Israeli nation had been constructed as a
sort of gateway by which the sparks of purity
would shine upon the whole of the human
race the world over. And these sparks multi-
ply daily, like one who gives to the treasurer,

until they are filled sufficiently, that is, until they develop to such an extent that they can understand the pleasantness and tranquility that are found in the kernel of love of others. For then they will know how to shift the balance to the right, and will place themselves under His burden, and the scale of sin will be eradicated from the world.

Baal HaSulam, "The *Arvut* [Mutual Guarantee]," Item 24

Know that a branch that extends from the internality is the people of Israel, which has been chosen as an operator of the general purpose and correction. It contains the preparation required for growing and developing until it moves the nations of the worlds, too, to achieve the common goal. The branch that extends from the externality is the nations of the world. They have not been imparted the qualities that make them worthy of receiving the development of the purpose one at a time. Rather, they are fit to receive the correction

155

at once and to the fullest, according to their Higher Root.

Baal HaSulam, "A Handmaid that Is Heir to Her Mistress"

The Israeli nation was to be a "transition." This means that to the extent that Israel cleanse themselves by keeping the Torah, so they pass their power on to the rest of the nations. And when the rest of the nations also sentence themselves to a scale of merit, then the Messiah will be revealed. That is because the role of the Messiah, is not only to qualify Israel to the ultimate goal of adhesion with Him, but to teach the ways of God to all the nations, as the verse says, "And all nations will flow onto Him."

Baal HaSulam,
"The Love for the Creator & Love for the Created Beings"

The revival of the nation is the foundation for the construction of the great repentance's, the repentance of the Upper Israel and the repentance of the whole world which will follow.

Rav Raiah Kook, *Orot HaTshuva* [*Lights of Repentance*] 17, 1

The role of the Israeli nation to qualify the world for a certain measure of purity, until they are worthy of taking upon themselves His work, no less than Israel were worthy at the time they received the Torah.

Baal HaSulam, "The *Arvut* [Mutual Guarantee]," Item 21

Judaism must present something new to the nations. That is what they expect from the return of Israel to the land! It is not in other teachings, for in that we never innovated; we were always their disciples. Rather, it is the wisdom of religion, justice and peace. In this, most nations are our disciples, and this wisdom is attributed to us alone.

Baal HaSulam, "The Solution"

The end of the correction of the world will only be by bringing all the people in the world under His work, as it is written, "And the Lord shall be King over all the earth; in that day shall the Lord be One, and His name one."

And the text specifies, "on that day," and not before. And there are several more verses, "for the earth shall be full of the knowledge of the Lord..." (*Isaiah*, 11:9) "...and all the nations shall flow on to him" (*Isaiah*, 2:2).

But the role of Israel towards the rest of the world resembles the role of our Holy Fathers towards the Israeli nation: just as the righteousness of our fathers helped us develop and cleanse until we became worthy of receiving the Torah, were it not for our fathers, who observed the whole of Torah before it was given, we would certainly not be any better than the rest of the nations.

Baal HaSulam, "The *Arvut* [Mutual Guarantee]," Item 20

Altruistic Communism (The religion of bestowal upon another) is seldom found in the human spirit; hence, the nobler people must take upon it to set an example for the entire world.

Baal HaSulam, "The Solution"

Each and every *Mitzva* that each person from Israel performs in order to bring contentment to one's Maker, and not for any self gratification, helps, to some extent, with the development of all the people of the world. This is because it is not done at once, but by slow, gradual development, until it increases to such a degree that it can bring all the people in the world to the desired purity.

Baal HaSulam, "The *Arvut* [Mutual Guarantee]," Item 20

Now it is upon us, relics, to correct that dreadful wrong. Each of us remainders should take upon himself, heart and soul, to henceforth intensify the internality of the Torah, and give it its rightful place, according to its merit over the externality of the Torah.

And then, each and every one of us will be rewarded with intensifying his own internality, meaning the Israel within us, which is the needs of the soul over our own externality, which is the Nations of the World within us, that is, the needs of the body. That force will come to the whole of Israel, until the Nations of the World within us recognize and acknowledge the merit of the great sages of Israel over them, and will listen to them and obey them.

...And they shall follow the words (Isaiah 14, 2), "And the people shall take them, and bring them to their place: and the house of Israel shall possess them in the land of the Lord." And also (Isaiah 49, 22), "And they shall bring thy sons in their arms, and thy daughters shall be carried on their shoulders." That is what is written in *The Zohar* (*Nasoh*, p 124b), "through this composition," which is *The Book of Zohar*, "they will be delivered from exile with mercy."

Baal HaSulam, "Introduction to The Book of Zohar," Item 71

Our sages said about the reason for the words: Therefore, the blessing of peace in the whole world precedes the strength, meaning the redemption, because "God did not find a vessel to hold the blessing for Israel but peace." Thus, as long as self-love and egoism exist among the nations, Israel, too, will not be able to serve the Creator in purity, as bestowal, as it is written in the explanation of the words, "And you shall be to me a kingdom of priests," in the essay, "The Arvut [mutual guarantee]." And we see it from experience, for the coming to the land and the building of the Temple could not persist and receive the blessings that God has sworn to our fathers.

And this is why they said, "God did not find a vessel to hold the blessing," meaning thus far Israel did not have a vessel to hold the blessing of the fathers. Therefore, the oath that we can inherit the land for all eternity has not yet been fulfilled, because world peace is the sole vessel that enables us to receive the blessing of the fathers, as in the prophecy of Isaiah.

Baal HaSulam, "The Peace"

Israel Must Carry Out
Their Role toward the World

Nothing in the world break the force of idol worshipping nations as when Israel engage in Torah. As long as Israel engage in Torah, the right intensifies and the power and might of the idol worshipping nations breaks ... When Israel do not engage in Torah, the left intensifies and the power of the idol worshipping nations—who nurse off the left—increases and they govern Israel and inflict upon them sentences they cannot endure. This is the reason why Israel were exiled and dispersed among the nations.

The Book of Zohar with the *Sulam* [Ladder] Commentary,
BeShalach, Items 305-306

In such a generation, all the destructors among the Nations of the World raise their heads and wish primarily to destroy and to kill the Children of Israel, as it is written (*Yevamot* 63), "No calamity comes to the world but for Israel." This means, as it is written in the above corrections, that they cause poverty, ruin, robbery, killing, and destruction in the whole world.

And through our many faults, we have witnessed to all that is said in the above-mentioned *Tikkunim* ... Now it is upon us, relics, to correct that dreadful wrong. Each of us remainders should take upon himself, heart and soul, to henceforth intensify the internality of the Torah, and give it its rightful place, according to its merit over the externality of the Torah.

Baal HaSulam, "Introduction to The Book of Zohar," Item 69

I have already given the gist of my views in 1933. I have also spoken to the leaders of the generation, but at the time, my words were not accepted, though I was screaming like a crane, warning about the destruction of the world. Alas, it made no impression.

Now, however, after the atom and hydrogen bombs, I think the world will believe me that the end of the world is coming rapidly, and Israel will be the first nation to burn, as in the previous war. Thus, today it is good to awaken the world to accept the only remedy, and they will live and persist.

Baal HaSulam, "The Solution"

But if, God forbid, it is to the contrary, and a person from Israel degrades the virtue of the internality of the Torah and its secrets, which deals with the conduct of our souls and their degrees, and the perception and the tastes of the *Mitzvot* with regard to the advantage of the externality of the Torah, which deals only with the practical part? Also, even if one does occasionally engage in the internality of the Torah, and dedicates a little of one's time to it, when it is neither night nor day, as though it were redundant, by that one dishonors and degrades the internality of the world, which are the Children of Israel, and enhances the externality of the world – meaning the Nations of the World – over them. They will humiliate and disgrace the Children of Israel, and regard Israel as superfluous, as though the world has no need for them, God forbid.

Furthermore, by that, they make even the externality in the Nations of the World overpower their own internality, for the worst among the Nations of the World, the harmful and the destructors of the world, rise above their internality, which are the Righteous of the Nations of the World. And then they make all the ruin and the heinous slaughter our generation had witnessed, may God protect us from here on.

Baal HaSulam, "Introduction to The Book of Zohar," Item 69

If they (Israel) accept the religion (bestowal upon others in the form of "Love thy friend as thyself"), the Temple can be built and the ancient glory restored. This would certainly prove to the nations, the rightness of Israel's return to their land, even to the Arabs. However, a secular return, such as today's, does not impress the nations whatsoever, and we must fear lest they will sell Israel's independence for their needs.

Baal HaSulam, "The Solution"

The redemption of Israel and the rise of Israel depend on the study of *The Zohar* and the internality of the Torah. And vise versa, all the destruction and the decline of the Children of Israel are because they have abandoned the internality of the Torah. They have degraded its merit and made it seemingly redundant.

Baal HaSulam, "Introduction to The Book of Zohar," Item 69

KABBALAH NOW

Proof that Our Generation Has Reached the Days of the Messiah

Our generation is the generation of the days of the Messiah. This is why we have been granted the redemption of our holy land from the hands of the foreigners. We have also been rewarded with the revelation of *The Book of Zohar*, which is the beginning of the realization of the verse, "And they shall teach no more every man his neighbor, and every man his brother, saying: 'Know the Lord,' for they shall all know Me, from the least of them unto the greatest of them" (Jeremiah 31).

Baal HaSulam, "A Speech for the Completion of *The Zohar*"

All the interpretations of *The Book of Zohar* before ours did not clarify as much as ten percent of the difficult places in *The Zohar*. And in the little they did clarify, their words are almost as abstruse as the words of *The Zohar* itself.

But in our generation we have been rewarded with the *Sulam* (Ladder) commentary, which is a complete interpretation of all the words of *The Zohar*. Moreover, not only does it not leave an unclear matter in the whole of *The Zohar* without interpreting it, but the clarifications are based on a straightforward analysis, which any intermediate student can understand. And since *The Zohar* appeared in our generation, it is a clear proof that we are already in the days of the Messiah, at the outset of that generation upon which it was said, "for the earth shall be full of the knowledge of the Lord."

Baal HaSulam, "A Speech for the Completion of *The Zohar*"

And who better than I knows that I am not at all worthy of being even a messenger and a scribe for disclosing such secrets, and much less to thoroughly understand them. And why has the Creator done so to me? It is only because the generation is worthy of it, as it is the last generation, which stands at the threshold of complete redemption. And for this reason, it is worthy of beginning to hear the voice of Messiah's *Shofar*, which is the revealing of the secrets, as has been explained.

Baal HaSulam, "Messiah's *Shofar* [horn]"

I am glad that I have been born in such a generation when it is permitted to disclose the wisdom of truth. And should you ask, "How do I know that it is permitted?" I will reply that I have been given permission to disclose. Until now, the ways by which it is possible to publicly engage and to fully explain each word have not been revealed to any sage ... And this is what the Creator has given me to the fullest extent. We deem it as dependent not on the greatness of the sage, but on the state of the generation, as our sages said, "Little Samuel was worthy, etc., but his generation was unworthy." This is why I said that my being rewarded with the manner of disclosing the wisdom is because of my generation.

Baal HaSulam, "The Teaching of the Kabbalah and Its Essence"

Since the whole of the wisdom of Kabbalah speaks of the revelation of the Creator, naturally, there is none more successful teaching for its task. This is what the Kabbalists aimed for—to arrange it so it is suitable for studying. And so they studied in it until the time of concealment (it was agreed to conceal it for a certain reason). However, this was only for a certain time, and not forever, as it is written in *The Zohar*, "This wisdom is destined to be revealed at the end of days, and even to children."

Baal HaSulam, "The Teaching of the Kabbalah and Its Essence"

The prohibition from Above to refrain from open study of the wisdom of truth was for a limited period, until the end of 1490. Thereafter is considered the last generation, in which the prohibition was lifted and permission has been granted to engage in *The Book of Zohar*. And since the year 1540, it has been a great *Mitzva* (precept) for the masses to study, old and young. And since the Messiah is bound to come as a result, and for no other reason, it is inappropriate to be negligent.

Rabbi Abraham Ben Mordechai Azulai, Introduction to the book, *Ohr HaChama [Light of the Sun]* 81

Rashbi and his generation, the authors of *The Zohar*, who were granted all 125 degrees in completeness, even though it was prior to the days of the Messiah. It was said about him and his disciples: "A sage is preferable to a prophet." Hence, we often find in *The Zohar* that there will be none like the generation of Rashbi until the generation of the Messiah King. This is why his composition made such a great impact in the world, since the secrets of the Torah in it occupy the level of all 125 degrees.

Hence, it is said in *The Zohar* that *The Book of Zohar* will be revealed only at the End of Days, the days of the Messiah. This is so because we have already said that if the degrees of the students are not at the full measure of the degree of the author, they will not understand his intimations, since they do not have a common attainment.

And since the degree of the authors of *The Zohar* is at the full level of the 125 degrees, they cannot be attained prior to the days of the Messiah. It follows that there will be no common attainment with the authors of *The Zohar* in the generations preceding the days of the Messiah. Hence, *The Zohar* could not be revealed in the generations before the generation of the Messiah.

Baal HaSulam, "A Speech for the Completion of The Zohar"

Trust and know, my brother, that the previous generations and the early days, those of the fifth millennium, are not as these generations and these days. In those days, the gates of the wisdom were closed and locked. Hence, then Kabbalists were only a few.

This is not so in this sixth millennium, when the gates of Lights, the gates of Mercy have been opened, since it is near the end of days. Now it is a joy of *Mitzva* (good deed) and great contentment in the eyes of the Creator to make the glory of His Kingdom known forever. Especially now, the holy writings of the Ari Luria have been printed, which opened for us the gates of Light that have been sealed and locked by a thousand keys since days of old, and all his words are words of the living God, based on Prophet Elijah, by whose permission he revealed what he revealed. Thus, now there is no obstacle or peril before us, just as with the revealed.

Rabbi Pinchas Eliahu Ben-Meir, *Sefer HaBrit*
[*Book of the Covenant*] Part 2, Essay no. 12, Chapter 5

When the days of the Messiah draw near, even infants in the world will find the secrets of the wisdom, knowing in them the end and

the calculations of redemption. At the same
time, it will be revealed to all.

The Book of Zohar with the *Sulam* [Ladder] Commentary,
VaYera, Item 460

An Opportunity for Redemption

Our generation is the generation of the days
of the Messiah. This is why we have been
granted the redemption of our holy land
from the hands of the foreigners. We have
also been rewarded with the revelation of *The
Book of Zohar*, which is the beginning of the
realization of the verse, "And they shall teach
no more every man his neighbor, and every
man his brother, saying, 'Know the Lord,' for
they shall all know Me, from the least of them
unto the greatest of them" (Jeremiah 31).

Yet, with those two, we have only been
rewarded with giving from the Creator, but
we have not received anything into our own
hands. Instead, we have been given a chance

to begin with the work of God, to engage in Torah and *Mitzvot Lishma*. Then we will be granted the great success that is promised to the generation of the Messiah, which all the generations before us did not know. And then we will be rewarded with the time of reception of both the complete attainment and the complete redemption.

Baal HaSulam, "A Speech for the Completion of The Zohar"

Even though the Creator has delivered the land from the hands of the nations and has given it to us, we have not yet received it. We are not enjoying it. But with this giving, the Creator has given us an opportunity for redemption, to be purified and sanctified and assume the work of God in Torah and *Mitzvot Lishma*. At that time, the Temple will be built and we will receive the land into our own authority. And then we will experience and feel the joy of redemption.

Baal HaSulam, "A Speech for the Completion of The Zohar"

Judaism must present something new to the nations. That is what they expect from the return of Israel to the land! It is not in other teachings, for in that we never innovated; we were always their disciples. Rather, it is the wisdom of religion, justice and peace. In this, most nations are our disciples, and this wisdom is attributed to us alone.

Baal HaSulam, "The Solution"

If they (Israel) accept the religion (bestowal upon others in the form of "Love thy friend as thyself"), the Temple can be built and the ancient glory restored. This would certainly prove to the nations, the rightness of Israel's return to their land, even to the Arabs. However, a secular return, such as today's, does not impress the nations whatsoever, and we must fear lest they will sell Israel's independence for their needs.

Baal HaSulam, "The Solution"

Now you will understand what is written *The Zohar*: "With this composition, the Children of Israel will be redeemed from exile." Also, in many other places, only through the expansion of the wisdom of Kabbalah in the masses will we obtain complete redemption.

They also said, "The Light in it reforms him." They were intentionally meticulous about it, to show us that only the Light enclosed within it, "like apples of gold in settings of silver," in it lies the cure that reforms a person. Both the individual and the nation will not complete the aim for which they were created, except by attaining the internality of the Torah and its secrets.

Baal HaSulam, "Introduction to the Book, Panim Meirot uMasbirot," Item 5

The redemption of Israel and the rise of Israel depend on the study of *The Zohar* and the internality of the Torah. And vise versa, all the destruction and the decline of the Children of Israel are because they have abandoned the internality of the Torah. They have degraded its merit and made it seemingly redundant.

Baal HaSulam, "Introduction to The Book of Zohar," Item 69

The Importance of Disseminating the Wisdom of Kabbalah

The prohibition from Above to refrain from open study of the wisdom of truth was for a limited period, until the end of 1490. Thereafter is considered the last generation, in which the prohibition was lifted and permission has been granted to engage in *The Book of Zohar*. And since the year 1540, it has been a great *Mitzva* (precept) for the masses to study, old and young. And since the Messiah is bound to come as a result, and for no other reason, it is inappropriate to be negligent.

Abraham Ben Mordechai Azulai, Introduction to the book, *Ohr HaChama [Light of the Sun]* 81

For a long time now, my conscience has burdened me with a demand to come out and create a fundamental composition regarding the essence of Judaism, religion, and the wisdom of Kabbalah, and spread it among the nation, so people will come to know and properly understand these exalted matters in their true meaning.

Baal HaSulam, "Time to Act"

Disclosure of the wisdom of the hidden in great masses, which is a necessary precondition that must be met prior to the complete redemption.

Baal HaSulam, "Messiah's *Shofar* [horn]"

Now you will understand what is written *The Zohar*: "With this composition, the Children of Israel will be redeemed from exile." Also, in many other places, only through the expansion of the wisdom of Kabbalah in the masses will we obtain complete redemption. They also said, "The Light in it reforms him." They were intentionally meticulous about it, to show us that only the Light enclosed within it, "like apples of gold in settings of silver," in it lies the cure that reforms a person. Both the individual and the nation will not complete the aim for which they were created, except by attaining the internality of the Torah and its secrets.

Baal HaSulam, "Introduction to the Book, Panim Meirot uMasbirot," Item 5

It is the great expansion of the wisdom of truth within the nation that we need first, so we may merit receiving the benefit from our Messiah. Consequently, the expansion of the wisdom and the coming of our Messiah are interdependent. Therefore, we must establish seminaries and compose books to hasten the distribution of the wisdom throughout the nation.

Baal HaSulam, "Introduction to the Book, Panim Meirot uMasbirot," Item 5

Not only are these secrets not forbidden to disclose, on the contrary, it is a great *Mitzva* [good deed] to disclose them (as written in *Pesachim* 119). And one who knows how to disclose and discloses them, his reward is plentiful. This is because on disclosing these

Lights to many, particularly to the many, depends the coming of Messiah soon in our days Amen.

Baal HaSulam, "Introduction to The Study of the Ten Sefirot," Item 30

It is written that each of the nations will hold a Jewish man and lead him to the Holy Land. And it was not enough that they could leave by themselves. You must understand from where the nations of the world would come by such a will and idea. Know that this is through the dissemination of the true wisdom, so they will evidently see the true God and the true law.

And the dissemination of the wisdom in the masses is called "a *Shofar*." Like the *Shofar*, whose voice travels a great distance, the echo of the wisdom will spread all over the world, so even the nations will hear and acknowledge that there is Godly wisdom in Israel.

Baal HaSulam, "Messiah's *Shofar* [horn]"

The current obligation to expand and consistently engage in the inner side of the Torah, in all its spiritual issues, which broadly include the general wisdom of Israel, whose peak is the knowledge of the Creator in truth, according to the depth of the secrets of Torah, requires clarification, scrutiny, and explanation, to make it increasingly clearer and more ubiquitous among our people.

Rav Raiah Kook,
Otzrot HaRaiah [Treasures of the Raiah], 2, 317

Be strong my friend, shining the Light of the concealed wisdom in the world. Now the days are near when all will know and recognize that the salvation of Israel and the salvation of the entire world depend only on the appearance of the wisdom of the hidden Light of the internality of the secrets of Torah in a clear language.

Rav Raiah Kook, Letters 1, 92

The great spiritual questions, which used to be solved only by the great and the excellent, must now be solved on different degrees for the entire nation, to lower exalted and sublime matters from the height of their tower to the depth of the common and ordinary. This requires tremendous and great richness of spirit along with constant, regular engagement, for only then the mind will expand and the language will be made clearer, to the point of expressing the deeper matters in a light and popular style, to revive thirsty souls.

Rav Raiah Kook, *Ikvei Ha'Tzon*, [*By the Footsteps of the Flock*], 54

The tendency of revealing the secrets of Torah is the ideal goal in life and in reality. The darkness, with which the contents of sanctity are covered, causes man's spirit to diminish, minimizing his aspirations. Thus, he is depleted, the whole of society weakens by the weakening of the individuals, and the nation becomes impoverished of spirit by the draining of its children's' spirit.

Rav Raiah Kook, *Orot HaKodesh* [*The Lights of Sanctity*] 1, 142

The tenor of life, is to attain adhesion with Him, strictly for the sake of benefitting the Creator, or to reward the public with achieving adhesion with Him.

Baal HaSulam, "The Solution"

THE BOOK OF ZOHAR

Rabbi Shimon Bar-Yochai and His Friends

Clearly, Rashbi composed *The Book of Zohar* according to the enlightenment that reached him while he was correcting in the cave ... It is a great and awe-inspiring composition, disclosing the secrets in greater depth than the Torah itself, and this is called revealing the Torah in its internality.

The Ramchal, *Adir BaMarom* [*The Mighty One on High*], 24

Only during the days of Rashbi, after 13 years of being in the cave, the gates of wisdom opened upon him, to shine for all of Israel through the end of days.

The Ramchal, *Adir BaMarom* [*The Mighty One on High*], 13

Rashbi and his generation, the authors of *The Zohar*, were granted all 125 degrees in completeness, even though it was prior to the days of the Messiah. It was said about him and his disciples: "A sage is preferable to a prophet." Hence, we often find in *The Zohar* that there will be none like the generation of Rashbi until the generation of the Messiah King. This is why his composition made such a great impact in the world, since the secrets of the Torah in it occupy the level of all 125 degrees.

Baal HaSulam, "A Speech for the Completion of *The Zohar*"

We would never have the power to strip the Torah of its clothing, were it not for Rashbi and his friends.

Ramak, *Know the God of Thy Father*, 16

And Rabbi Shimon Bar-Yochai would reveal the secrets of the Torah, and his friends listened to his voice, joining him in this composition, each answering his part. Just as the *Mishnah* was written by the *Tana'im*, where our Rabbi combined all of their thoughts and made them into The Book of the Mishnah.

Likewise, Rabbi Shimon Bar-Yochai wanted a book to be written that comprises all the essays of the students in his seminary, that the book would be composed regarding the Torah. For the compositions speak of individual matters, but *The Zohar*, which was made regarding the Torah, is call "the great opening of the entirety of the Torah." And here, Rabbi Shimon Bar-Yochai instructed Rabbi Abba to be the writer and organizer of all the words that the sages, students of the seminary would say, whenever and wherever they are, to arrange everything according to the order of the Torah.

The Ramchal, *Adir BaMarom* [*The Mighty One on High*], 24

The Importance of The Book of Zohar

And this book shall be called *The Book of Zohar* due to the influence of that Light from the Upper Radiance [*Zohar*]. Through its Light, all who engage in it impart by Divine

Providence, for the Upper Light and abundance above the reason would was imparted in the secrets of the Torah. Since it flowed from there, this composition was called *The Book of Zohar*, meaning that it extended from that *Zohar* [Radiance].

Ramak , *Know the God of Thy Father*, 2

Because Israel is destined to taste from the Tree of Life, which is the holy *Book of Zohar*, through it, they will be redeemed from exile.

Rabbi Shimon Bar-Yochai, *The Book of Zohar*,
Portion *Naso*, Item 90

The redemption of Israel and the rise of Israel depend on the study of *The Zohar* and the internality of the Torah.

Baal HaSulam, "Introduction to The Book of Zohar," Item 69

This point in time requires accelerated acquisition of the inner Torah. *The Book of Zohar* breaks new paths, makes a highway in the desert, the *Zohar* and all it harvests are ready to open the doors of redemption.

The Rav Raiah Kook, *Orot [Lights]*, 57

One who has not seen the Light of *The Book of Zohar*, has never seen Light.

The Rav Tzvi Hirsh of Ziditshov,
Ateret Tzvi [A Crown of Glory] Parashat BeHaalotcha

When engaging in this composition, one evokes the power of the souls with the power of Moses. This is so because while engaging in it, they renew the generated Light, which was created during its composition. And Divinity shines and illuminates from that Light as when it was first created. And all who engage in it reawaken that same benefit and that first Light, which Rashbi and his friends had revealed while composing.

Ramak, *Ohr Yakar [Precious Light]*, Gate 1, Item 5

It is known that the study of *The Zohar* is capable indeed. Know that the study of *The Zohar*, creates desire, and the words of *The Zohar* strongly evoke to the work of the Creator.

Rabbi Nachman of Braslev,
Sichot HaRan [Talks of Rabbi Nachman], 108

He also said that he asked his rav to be saved from pride and constantly pleaded to him about that. He told him "Study *The Zohar*," and he replied, "I am studying *The Zohar*." And his rav replied, "Study *The Zohar* a great deal."

Rav Pinchas Shapira of Koritz, *Midrash Pinchas*, 36, Item 73

The virtue of the study of *The Book of Zohar* is already known, as the Ari said, "A single day of studying *The Book of Zohar* and the secrets of Torah equals an entire year of studying the literal.

"Introduction to The Zohar," Livorno Press, 1892

There is no comparison between the livelihood and delight in the study of the revealed and the study of *The Zohar* and the corrections. And he said about himself that he has no livelihood and delight even in the study of Gemarah, compared to *The Zohar* and the corrections.

Rav Pinchas Shapira of Koritz, *Midrash Pinchas*, 72, Item 3

The language of *The Zohar* remedies the soul, even when one does not understand what it says at all. It is similar to one who enters a perfumery; even when he does not take a thing, he still absorbs the fragrance.

Rabbi Moshe Chaim Ephraim of Sudilkov, *Degel Machaneh Ephraim [The Banner of the Camp of Ephraim]*, Excerpts

There is no measurement or value to the virtue of the study of the words of the Living God in *The Book of Zohar* and all that accompany it, and the words of true sages, and especially the clear writings of the Ari ... By constant engagement, the gates of Light and the openings of wisdom will be revealed to all who walk the path of the Creator wholeheartedly, whose soul craves to draw near to the hall of the honorable King, the one who lives forever. Hence, all who volunteer to engage in it even an hour or two each day, are blessed.

The Creator adds a good thought to an act, and it will be regarded as though he is standing all day long, forever, in the court of the Creator, and his dwelling place is in the secrets of the Torah.

Rav Raiah Kook, *Love of Israel in Sanctity*, 232

Hear me my brothers and companions, the friends, who are craving and seeking the truth, the truth of the work of the heart—to behold the pleasantness of the Creator and to visit His Hall: My soul shall bend and cling unto *The Book of Zohar*, as the power of engaging in the holy book is known from our ancient sages.

Rabbi Tzvi Hirsh Eichenstein of Ziditshov,
Sur MeRa [Depart from Evil], p 4

The livelihood of the person of Israel depends on *The Book of Zohar*, studying with joy and pleasantness, and with fear and love, each one according to his attainment and sanctity, and all of Israel are holy.

Rav Yitzhak Yehuda Yehiel Safrin of Komarno,
Notzer Hesed [Keeping Mercy], Chapter 4, Teaching 20

The honor and the virtue of studying *The Zohar* are already known: they cancel all sorts of tragedies and harsh and bad decrees.
The Rabbis of Jerusalem, 1921

Each and every letter in *The Book of Zohar* and the writings of our great teacher, the Rav Chaim Vital ... are great corrections for the soul, to correct all the incarnations.
Rav Yitzhak Yehuda Yehiel Safrin of Komarno,
Notzer Hesed [Keeping Mercy], Chapter 4, Teaching 20

Know that the entire Book of *Zohar* and the obligation to study it etc., is all a positive *Mitzva* [commandment to do a certain action], to cleave to it and to know that God is found, in sacred knowledge in the particular and in the unifications, and with love, fear, and unity.
Rav Yitzhak Yehuda Yehiel Safrin of Komarno, *Netiv Mitzvotecha*
[*The Path of Your Commandments*], Path 2, Item 3

My sons and my brothers, accustom yourselves to delve into the study the words of *The Zohar* and the corrections. One who has never seen the Light of *The Zohar*, sweeter than honey, has never seen Lights in his life, and has never tasted the flavor of the Torah. Moreover, it purifies the soul and cleanses it. Even a mere utterance through the lips is a great remedy and correction for the soul. In particular, the book of corrections, which are the actual corrections of the soul from any flaw, blemish, and disease.

Rav Yitzhak Yehuda Yehiel Safrin of Komarno,
"Introduction to Atzei Eden [Trees of Eden]"

My teacher (the Ari), gave Rabbi Abraham Ha-Levi good advice pertaining to attainment—to study *The Zohar* only for knowledge, without deep study, forty or fifty pages each day, and to read *The Book of Zohar* many times.

Rav Chaim Vital, *The Writings of the Ari*,
"The Gate of the Holy Spirit"

The livelihood of the person of Israel depends on *The Book of Zohar* and the writings of the Ari, studying with joy and pleasantness, and with fear and love, each according to his attainment and sanctity, and all of Israel are holy.

Rav Yitzhak Yehuda Yehiel Safrin of Komarno,
Notzer Hesed [Keeping Mercy], Chapter 4, Teaching 20

"And the wise shall shine as the brightness of the firmament" are the authors of the Kabbalah. They are the ones who exert in this brightness, called *The Book of Zohar*, which is like Noah's ark, gathering two from a town, and seven kingdoms, and sometimes one from a town and two from a family, in whom the words, "Every son that is born you shall cast into the Nile" come true. The Torah is called "a son." The newborn is the attained. "Into the Nile" means the light of Torah. "Cast" is like "You will study it" [a Hebrew anagram], where you study each insight that is born in you by the light of Torah and by its soul. This is the light of this *Book of Zohar*.

The Book of Zohar with the *Sulam* [Ladder] Commentary,
BeHaalotcha, Item 88

The reason why our sages wrote that the study of *The Zohar* is awe-inspiring and exalted ... in all the Torah there is *PARDESS* and in all the studies, the concealed is not apparent whatsoever. On the contrary, a reader who repeats only the literate does not understand that there is a secret to the Torah at all. This is not so in *The Book of Zohar*, in which the secrets are open and the disciple knows that it speaks of the wonders and secrets of the Torah, which he does not know, and this is very instrumental for the correction of the soul.

Rabbi Chaim of Voluzhin,
Nefesh HaChaim [*The Soul of Life*], Set no. 7

A new Light is renewed every moment, until it actually becomes a new creation, through *The Zohar* and our teacher the Ari.

Heichal HaBracha [The Hall of Blessing],
Devarim [*Deuteronomy*], p 11

To excite the hearts of Israel to Torah and to work in the wisdom of internality, which is sweeter than honey and nectar, opens the eyes, and revives the soul, hidden delight, sweet as the light to the eyes, and good for the soul, refining and illuminating it with good and upright qualities, tasting the flavor of the hidden Light of the next world in this world through the wisdom of *The Zohar*.

Rav Yitzhak Yehuda Yehiel Safrin of Komarno, *Netiv Mitzvotecha* [*The Path of Your Commandments*], Introduction

Studying *The Zohar* ... builds worlds. It is all the more so if one is rewarded with studying and understanding the meaning of an article. It will correct him in an hour more than the study of the literal will do in a year.

Rabbi Shalom Ben Moshe Buzzaglo, *The King's Throne*, Tikkun [Correction] 43, Item 60

I answered a scholar who asked about the writings of the students of the Ari, that the study of *The Zohar* is a great correction with which to illuminate the soul and to sanctify it. The Ari gave this correction to a one who was repenting to study five pages of *The Zohar* each day, even though he did not know what it was saying, for that reading illuminates the soul and corrects it. It seems that the study of *The Zohar* specifically has that power, more than the study of Mishnah, Talmud and Bible, and it is a wonder, the way its power is greater than the entire Torah, whether it is the Bible or the Mishnah, etc., those are his words.

And I told him that undoubtedly, any study of the Torah is exalted and uplifting, particularly if it is truly *Lishma* [for Her name]. Surely, it builds its ascensions in heaven and corrects the worlds and unites the beloved. Still, the greatness of the study of *The Zohar* is that the Bible, the Mishnah, and the Talmud are excessively clothed, and the concealed is completely indiscernible in them. *The Zohar*, however, speaks explicitly of the secrets of Torah, and even the most illiterate reader will realize that its words stem from the depths of the secrets of Torah. Thus, as the secrets of the Torah are revealed and unclothed, they illuminate and radiate the soul.

The Chida, *Shem HaGedolim* [*The Name of the Great Ones*], "Books," System no. 2

Torah and Mitzvot

Torah

The Torah is Simple Light that expands from His Essence, whose sublimity is endless.

Baal HaSulam, "Introduction to the book, From the Mouth of a Sage"

The Torah being all the Names of the Creator, which belong to the creatures.

Baal HaSulam, "The Acting Mind"

The word Torah comes from the word *Horaa* [instruction] and from the word *Maraa* [showing] and *Reiah* [vision], meaning complete awareness that leaves no filaments in its wake.

Baal HaSulam, Letter no. 11

Torah refers to the Light *clothed* in the Torah, meaning, as our sages said, "I have created

the evil inclination, I have created the Torah
as a spice." This refers to the Light in it, since
the Light in it reforms it.

Baal HaSulam, *Shamati [I Heard]*, article no. 6,
"Support in the Torah"

The Torah is the only spice to annul and
subdue the evil inclination, as our sages said,
"The Light in it reformed them."

Baal HaSulam, "The Teaching of the Kabbalah and Its Essence"

Mitzvot

The *Mitzva* is the *Kli* (vessel) where the Light
is clothed, meaning a Holy Name that belongs specifically to that *Mitzva*. This is the
meaning of "The *Mitzva* is a candle and the
Torah is Light."

Baal HaSulam, "Introduction to the book,
From the Mouth of a Sage"

Mitzvot are called *Mitzva* [commandment]
after the *Dvekut* [adhesion], for attaches the
Godly part within one to the entire *Ein Sof*,

from the word *Tzavta* (together).

Rabbi Menahem Nachum Twersky of Chernobyl,
Maor Einayim [Light of the Eyes], *VaYera*

The primary reward from the *Mitzva* [commandment] is the *Metzaveh* [the commander], which is the Godly adhesion and the spiritual delight in carrying out the *Mitzva*, which is the reception of the face of Divinity. Without that, it would be called *Mitzva* vacuously, for it would be without vitality or soul, and would only be the body of the *Mitzva*. Indeed, it is called "a *Mitzva*" only for the passion and the adhesion of the Godly part that dwells within to the Root, with all the parts of Israel. It is known that in every Godly work, both in speech and in action, there are body and soul, reviving that speech or that action. Without it, it would have no livelihood. This is why the wicked in their lives are called "dead," for their actions are devoid of livelihood.

Rabbi Menahem Nachum Twersky of Chernobyl,
Maor Einayim [Light of the Eyes], *VaYera*

There are 613 Mitzvot, and in each Mitzva a light of a unique degree is deposited, which corresponds to a unique organ in the 613 organs and tendons of the souls and the body. It follows that while performing the Mitzva, one extends to the corresponding organ in his soul and body, the degree of light that belongs to that organ and tendon.

Rabash, *Rabash—the Social Writings*,
"The Importance of a Prayer of Many"

The Essence of the Work in Torah and Mitzvot

One should crave being awarded the reward of a Mitzva (commandment/good deed). This means that through keeping the Mitzvot he will be rewarded with adherence to the Metzaveh (Commander).

Baal HaSulam, *Shamati [I Heard]*, Article no. 227,
"The Reward for a Mitzva–a Mitzva"

When one can aim in order to bestow, this act is called "a Mitzva [good deed]."

Rabash, *The Rungs of the Ladder*,
"Concerning the Reward of the Receivers"

The work in Torah and Mitzvot begins primarily after one has been awarded repentance from love. Only then is it possible to engage in Torah and Mitzvot with love and fear, as we are commanded.

Baal HaSulam, "Introduction to The Study of the Ten Sefirot," Item 133

All the Mitzvot that are written in the Torah or the accepted ones, which the Patriarchs established, although they are mostly actions or words, they are all to correct the heart, "for the Lord searches all hearts, and understands all the inclinations of the thoughts."

Rav Abraham Eben Ezra, *Yesod Morah*, p 8b

These were the words of our sages (*Beresheet Rabba* 44) when they asked, "Why should the Creator mind whether one slaughters at the throat or at the back of the neck?" After all, the *Mitzvot* were given only to cleanse people, and that cleansing means the cleansing of the turbid body, which is the purpose that emerges from the observation of all the Torah and *Mitzvot*.

Baal HaSulam, *Matan Torah* [The Giving of the Torah], Item 12

Our sages said, "The Torah and *Mitzvot* were given only so as to cleanse Israel." This is the cleansing of the body until one attains a second nature defined as "love for others," meaning the one *Mitzva*: "Love thy friend as thyself," which is the final aim of the Torah, after which one immediately attains *Dvekut* with Him.

Baal HaSulam, *Matan Torah* [The Giving of the Torah], Item 15

If one's intention in the Torah and *Mitzvot* is not to benefit the Creator, but oneself, not only will the nature of the will to receive in him not be inverted, but rather, the will to receive in him will be much more than what he was given by the nature of his creation.

Baal HaSulam, "A Speech for the Completion of *The Zohar*"

The purpose of the study of Torah is to come to feel the Giver of the Torah. If one does not place the goal of reaching the Giver of the Torah before one's eyes, he is considered "a gentile," meaning he has no need for faith, that is, to have a need to seek advice for achieving faith. This is why he is still regarded as "a gentile" and not as "Israel."

Rabash, *The Rungs of the Ladder*,
"What are Torah and Work on the Path of the Creator"

The purpose of the whole Creation is that the lowly creatures will be able, by keeping Torah and *Mitzvot*, to rise ever upward, ever developing, until they are rewarded with *Dvekut* with their Creator.

Baal HaSulam, *Matan Torah* [The Giving of the Torah], Item 6

The whole of the Torah and the *Mitzvot* were given for the sole purpose of cleansing Israel, which is the cleansing of the body, after which he will be granted the true reward, which is *Dvekut* with Him, the purpose of Creation.

Baal HaSulam, The *Arvut* [Mutual Guarantee], Item 27

By accustoming themselves to keeping Torah and the *Mitzvot* in order to bring contentment to their Maker, they gradually depart from the bosom of the natural creation and acquire a second nature, being love of others.

Baal HaSulam, *Matan Torah* [The Giving of the Torah], Item 13

The Creator gave us Torah and *Mitzvot*, which we were commanded to do only in order to bestow contentment upon the Creator. Had it not been for the engagement in Torah and *Mitzvot Lishma* (for Her Name), to bring contentment to the Creator with them, and not to benefit ourselves, there would have been no tactic in the world that could help us invert our nature.

Baal HaSulam, "A Speech for the Completion of The Zohar"

By keeping Torah and *Mitzvot*, the purpose of creation—to do good to His creations—becomes revealed.

Rabash, *Rabash—the Social Writings*, "The Importance of a Prayer of Many"

The meaning of the souls of the children of Israel is that they are a part of God Above. The soul cascaded by way of cause and consequence and descended degree-by-degree until it became suitable to come into this world and clothe the filthy corporeal body.

By keeping the Torah and observing its *Mitzvot*, it ascends degree-by-degree until its stature is completed, and it is fit to receive its reward from The Whole. This has been prepared for it in advance, meaning attaining the holy Torah by way of the Names of the Creator, which are the 613 deposits.

> Baal HaSulam, "Introduction to the book,
> From the Mouth of a Sage"

613 Suggestions and 613 Deposits

There are two parts in Torah and *Mitzvot*.

A. The Torah and *Mitzvot* as they appear to all, being the keeping of *Mitzvot* and the study of Torah in the form of 613 counsels. These have the power to purify and cleanse the body, and enhance the merit of the soul, to be worthy and merit receiving the Light of the King's face, as the soul was in its root, before it diminished and came into this base body in the base world.

B.   Keeping the Mitzvot and studying the Torah in the form of 613 deposits, namely the matter of attaining His Names and the full reward of the souls.

The merit of the latter part over the former is as the merit of Heaven over Earth. This is because the first part is mere preparation, and the second part is the actual completeness and the purpose of Creation.

Baal HaSulam, "Introduction to the book, From the Mouth of a Sage"

In several places in *The Zohar*, he calls the 613 Mitzvot, "613 counsels" and in many other places in *The Zohar* he calls the 613 Mitzvot,

"613 deposits." This is so because at first, one must keep the Torah and the Mitzvot in order to purify his body and enhance his soul. At that time, the 613 Mitzvot are as 613 counsels for him, "suggestions" by which to gradually purify and be awarded coming before the King, and receiving the Light of his face. This is because keeping Torah and Mitzvot gradually purify him, until he is rewarded with the Light of the King's face.

Also, it is written similarly in the Gemarah: "The Creator cares not if one slaughters at the throat or slaughters at the back of the neck? Rather, we were given the Torah and Mitzvot only to purify Israel."

However, after one has been sufficiently purified and merits the Light of the King's face, one's eyes and soul open and he is awarded the attaining the 613 Sacred Lights found in the 613 Mitzvot. These are His Holy Names, the ones he can attain.

By keeping each of the *Mitzvot*, one takes the part of the Light deposited in that *Mitzva*, since the *Mitzva* is a *Kli* (vessel) where the Light is clothed, meaning a Holy Name that belongs specifically to that *Mitzva*. This is the meaning of "The *Mitzva* is a candle and the Torah—Light." At that time, he calls the 613 *Mitzvot* "613 commandments (deposits)."

Baal HaSulam, "Introduction to the book,
From the Mouth of a Sage"

We should keep the Torah and *Mitzvot* so it will bring us into purity. Purity means purification of the *Kelim* [vessels] from the will to receive for oneself, which is called "dirt," for it is in disparity of form from the Creator, who is all about bestowal. Hence prior to cleaning the *Kelim*, it is impossible to place anything good in them because anything that is placed in a dirty *Kli* [vessel] will be spoiled.

Therefore, we must seek good advice for things that will purify our *Kelim*. This is called "qualification and preparation to be able to receive the delight and pleasure." And because of that, we were given 613 *Mitzvot*, which *The Zohar* calls, "613 counsels." These are suggestions on how to purify ourselves from the filth of our vessels of reception.

It is written in the Introduction of The Book of Zohar" (p 242), "*The Zohar* calls the *Mitzvot* in the Torah, 'deposits.' However, they 're also called 'counsels.' The difference between them is that there are front and back in everything. The preparation for something is called 'back," and the attainment of that thing is called 'front.' Similarly, in Torah and *Mitzvot* there is 'We shall do,' and 'We shall hear.' When keeping the Torah and *Mitzvot* by way of 'Who do His words,' before they are rewarded with hearing, the *Mitzvot* are called '613 counsels,' and they are considered 'back.' And when rewarded with hearing the voice of His word, the *Mitzvot* become deposits, from the word "deposited."

Rabash, *The Rungs of the Ladder*, "Holiness and Purity in the Work"

The language of *The Zohar* calls the *Mitzvot* [commandments] in the Torah 613 deposits. However, it is also called 613 suggestions. The difference between them is that everything has anterior and posterior. The preparation for something is called "posterior," and the attainment something is called "anterior."

Accordingly, Torah and *Mitzvot* have the aspect of doing and the aspect of hearing, as our sages wrote (*Shabbat* 88), "Who carry out His word, hearing the voice of His word," doing first and hearing afterward. The *Mitzvot* are called 613 suggestions, and they are considered "posterior," and when rewarded with hearing the voice of His word, the 613 *Mitzvot* become deposits, from the term "deposit," since there are 613 *Mitzvot*, and in each *Mitzva*, Light is deposited from a specific degree, corresponding to a specific organ of the 613 organs and tendons of the soul and of the body.

Rabash, *The Rungs of the Ladder*,
"What Is a Half of a Shekel, in the work (1)"

It is known that the meaning of the souls of the children of Israel is that they are a part of God Above. The soul cascaded by way of cause and consequence and descended degree-by-degree until it became suitable to come into this world and clothe the filthy corporeal body.

By keeping the Torah and observing its Mitzvot, it ascends degree-by-degree until its stature is completed, and it is fit to receive its reward from The Whole. This has been prepared for it in advance, meaning attaining the holy Torah by way of the Names of the Creator, which are the 613 deposits.

Baal HaSulam, "Introduction to the Book, From the Mouth of a Sage"

The Torah Develops the Recognition of Evil in a Person

When one engages in the Torah, one feels one's remoteness to the extent of one's exertion.

Baal HaSulam, *Shamati* [*I Heard*], Article no. 56,
"Torah is Called Indication"

For engaging in *Mitzvot*, and the work to bring contentment to our Maker rapidly develops that sense of recognition of evil.

Baal HaSulam "The Essence of Religion and Its Purpose"

The Torah and the *Mitzvot* were given only to purify Israel, to develop in us the sense of recognition of evil, imprinted in us at birth, which is generally defined as our self-love, and to come to the pure good defined as the "love of others," which is the one and only passage to the love of God.

Baal HaSulam, "The Freedom"

The beginning of one's work is the recognition of evil. This means that a person asks of the Creator to feel how bad he is, meaning the will to receive. Knowing it—that the will to receive is called "evil"—is something that only the Creator can make him feel. This is considered that through the Torah, one can achieve recognition of evil, meaning to know how evil the will to receive is. Afterwards, he can ask for the will

to receive to be replaced and to be given the desire to bestow in return for it.
Rabash, *The Rungs of the Ladder*, "Holiness and Purity in the Work"

When one engages in the Torah, he sees the truth, meaning one's measure of remoteness from spirituality, and one sees that he is such a low creature, that there is not a worse person on earth than him.
Baal HaSulam, *Shamati* [*I Heard*], Article no. 56, "Torah is Called Indication"

What should one do in order to come to love the Creator? For that purpose we are granted the remedy of engaging in Torah and *Mitzvot*, for the Light in it reforms. There is Light there, which lets one feel the severity of the state of separation. And slowly, as one intends to acquire the Light of Torah, hatred for separation is created in him. He begins to feel the reason that causes him and his souls to be separated and far from the Creator.
Baal HaSulam, *Shamati* [*I Heard*], Article no. 34, "The Profit of a Land"

What is the essence of that development, which is attained through Torah and *Mitzvot*?

Bear in mind that it is the recognition of the evil within us. That engagement in *Mitzvot* can slowly and gradually purify those who delve in them. And the scale by which we measure the degrees of cleansing is the measurement of the recognition of the evil within us.

Baal HaSulam, "The Essence of Religion and Its Purpose"

Since he had learned a lot of Torah, through it he was granted seeing the truth about the distance between him and the Creator, meaning the measure of his remoteness and nearness. This is the meaning of his mind being crude, meaning that he saw the complete form of one who is proud, which is his will to receive, and then he could see the truth that it was him who was most ugly. How did he see the truth? By learning much Torah.

Thus, how will he be able to cleave to Him, since he is such an ugly person? This is the reason why he asked if all the people were as ugly as him, or that he was the only ugly one but the rest of the people in the world were not ugly.

What was the answer? "I don't know." It means that that they do not feel, hence they do not know. And why do they not feel? It is for the simple reason that they were not rewarded with seeing the truth, since they lack Torah, so the Torah will show them the truth.

To that Elijah replied to him: "go to the craftsman who made me," because he saw that he had come into a state from which he could not ascend. For this reason Elijah appeared and told him, "go to the craftsman who made me." In other words, since the Creator created you so ugly, He must have known that it is with these *Kelim* (Vessels) that the goal can be achieved.

Baal HaSulam, *Shamati [I Heard]*, Article no. 56,
"Torah is Called Indication"

Through the subtle pleasantness we feel when working sincerely to Him, to please Him, there develops within us a relative recognition of the lowliness of these sparks of self-love—that they are obstacles on our way to receiving that subtle taste of bestowal upon the Creator.

Baal HaSulam, "The Essence of Religion and Its Purpose"

If one engages in Torah and *Mitzvot*, even for one's own pleasure, still, through the light in it, he will feel the terrible inferiority and depravity in the nature of reception for oneself. At that time, he will devote his heart to retiring from this nature of reception and will completely dedicate himself to working only to bestow contentment upon his Maker. Then the Creator will open his eyes and will show him a world that is utterly perfect.

Rabash, *The Rungs of the Ladder*, "There Is an Appointee Above Who Strikes Him and Tells Him, 'Grow,' in the Work."

What Is a Prayer?

One does not call upon the Creator loudly, but discreetly, from the heart and from his internality.

Rabbi Menahem Mendel of Kotzk

A request is something that a person feels that he is lacking. It is in the heart. It makes no difference what he says, since "a request" means that one asks for what he lacks, and all of one's wants are not in the mouth, but in the heart. Therefore, it makes no difference what a person says, but the Creator knows the thoughts. Hence, Above, only what the heart demands is heard, not what the mouth demands, for the above reason that the mouth is not deficient and needs to be satisfied.

Rabash, *The Rungs of the Ladder*, "What is, 'A Woman Who Inseminates First, Gives Birth to a Male,' in the Work"

The prayer must be a *whole* prayer, that is, from the bottom of the heart. It means that one knows one hundred percent that there is no one in the world who can help him but the Creator Himself.

Yet, how does one know that, that there is no one to help him but the Creator Himself? One can acquire that awareness precisely if he has exerted all the powers at his disposal and it did not help him. Thus, one must do every possible thing in the world to attain "for the Creator." Then one can pray from the bottom of one's heart, and then the Creator hears his prayer.

Baal HaSulam, *Shamati [I Heard]*, Article no. 5, "Lishma Is an Awakening from Above"

Since half a thing is not given from Above, one must pray to the Creator to give him complete help. This means that during one's prayer—when he arranges what is in his heart, since a prayer is work in the heart—one must decide for himself that he wishes for the Creator to give him a desire to annul before Him altogether, leaving no desire under his own authority, but that all the desires will be only to glorify the Creator. And when he decides on complete annulment, he asks of the Creator to help him carry it out ... This is called "a complete prayer," since his desire is for the Creator to give him a complete desire, without any compromises for himself, and he asks of the Creator to help him always be with His righteousness.

Rabash, Letter no. 65

The Lord is near to the brokenhearted.

Psalms, 34

What does it mean that 'The Lord heals the brokenhearted'? It is known that man's essence is his heart. The heart is the *Kli* [vessel] that receives the *Kedusha* [holiness] from Above, as we learn concerning the breaking of the vessels—if the *Kli* is broken, anything that is placed in it will leak out.

Similarly, if the heart is broken and the will to receive governs the heart, the abundance cannot enter it because everything that the will to receive receives goes out to the *Klipot* [shells]. This is called "the breaking of the heart." Hence, when one prays to the Creator and says, "You must help me because I am worse than everyone else, since I feel that the will to receive is governing my heart, hence nothing of *Kedusha* can enter my heart. I want no luxuries, but simply to be able to do something in order to bestow, and I simply cannot. Therefore, only You can save me."

By that, we can interpret what is written (Psalm, 34), "The Lord is near to the brokenhearted," to those people who ask of the Creator to help them make their hearts unbroken, but rather whole.

Rabash, *The Rungs of the Ladder*,
"Return O Israel unto the Lord Your God"

There is no happier state in a man's world than when he finds himself despaired with his own powers, meaning that he has already toiled and did everything he could possibly do, but there is no cure. This is so because at that time, he is worthy of a whole prayer for His help, for he knows for certain that his own work will not yield him the benefit. As long as he feels that he has some power of his own for the work, his prayer is not whole, since the evil inclination rushes in and tells him that first, he must do all that he can, and then he will be desirable to the Creator.

It is said about that, "The Lord is high and the low will see." After one has exerted in all sorts of labors and has become disillusioned, he arrives at a point of true lowliness. He knows that he is the lowest of all people because there is nothing in his entire body that is good. At that time, his prayer is whole and he is answered by His generous hand. The writing says about that, "And the people of Israel sighed because of the labor ... and their cry rose.

Baal HaSulam, Letter no. 57

By not being able to exit the will to receive for oneself and feeling needy of the Creator's help, a need is born within for the Creator's assistance. And His help is through the Torah, since the light in it reforms him, meaning he receives vessels of bestowal.

Rabash, *The Rungs of the Ladder*,
"What Is the Basis upon which Holiness Is Built"

From one's praying to Him, to draw him near by *Dvekut* (Adhesion), called "equivalence of form," discerned as the annulment of the will to receive to be in order to bestow. The Creator says about that, "My sons defeated Me." That is, I gave you the will to receive, and you ask of Me to give you a will to bestow instead.

Baal HaSulam, *Shamati* [*I Heard*], Article no. 19,
"What Is the Creator Hates the Bodies, in the Work"

There are three conditions in prayer:
1. Believing that He can save him, although he has the worst conditions of all his contemporaries, still, "Is the Lord's hand

waxed short" from saving him? If not, then "the Landlord cannot save His vessels."

2. He no longer has any counsel, that he has already done all that he could, but saw no cure to his plight.

3. If He does not help him, he will be better off dead than alive. Prayer is the lost in the heart. The more he is lost, so is the measure of his prayer. Clearly, one who lacks luxuries is not like one who has been sentenced to death, and only the execution is missing, and he is already tied with iron chains, and he stands and begs for his life. He will certainly not rest or sleep or be distracted for even a moment from praying for his life.

Baal HaSulam, *Shamati* [*I Heard*], Article no. 209,
"Three Conditions in Prayer"

When one goes to pray to the Creator to help him, he must first prepare and examine himself, to see what he has and what he is missing, and then he can know for what to ask the Creator's help. This is the meaning of the words, "Out of the depths I have called upon You, O Lord." "Depth" means that a person is in the lowest possible state, as it is written, "Depths of the nether-world," meaning his deficiency is below and he feels that he is beneath all other people.

In other words, he feels so remote from *Kedusha* [holiness], more than all other people, meaning that no one feels the truth, that his body has no connection to *Kedusha*. Hence, those people who do not see the truth—that they are remote from *Kedusha*—can be satisfied with their work in the holy work. But he is suffering from the state he is in.

Rabash, *The Rungs of the Ladder*, "What is, 'A Woman Who Inseminates First, Gives Birth to a Male,' in the Work"

We should understand what our sages said, "One does not find himself in debt" (*Shabbat*, 119). Accordingly, one cannot correct his actions, for he will never see that his actions are corrupt and require correction. Thus, one must always remain corrupt.

The thing is that it is known that man was created with a nature of wanting only to delight himself. Therefore, in everything he learns, he wishes to learn how he can enjoy. Thus, if a person wishes to enjoy, he will naturally avoid learning other things than what his heart desires, for this is his nature.

For this reason, one who wishes to draw near to the Creator and to learn things that show ways by which to bestow upon the Creator, must pray to the Creator to give him a different heart, as it is written, "Create for me a pure heart, O God." This means that when he has another heart, when the desire in the heart is a desire to bestow, then in everything he learns, he will naturally see ways that show only how to bestow upon the Creator.

However, he will never see against the heart. It is said about that, "And I will remove the stony heart from within you, and I will give you a heart of flesh.

Rabash, Steps of the Ladder,
"One Learns Only where One's Heart Desires"

When concealment overpowers one and he comes to a state where the work becomes tasteless, and he cannot picture and feel any love and fear, and he cannot do anything in holiness, then his only counsel is to cry to the Creator to take pity on him and remove the screen from his eyes and heart.

The issue of crying is a very important one. It is as our sages write: "all the gates were locked except for the gates of tears." The world asks about that: If the gates of tears are not locked, what is the need for the gates at all?... Thus, when were the gates of tears not locked? Precisely when all the gates were locked. It is then that there is room for the gates of tears and then one sees that they were not locked.

However, when the gates of prayer are open, the gates of tears and weeping are irrelevant. This is the meaning of the gates of tears being locked. Thus, when are the gates of tears not locked? Precisely when all the gates are locked, the gates of tears are open. This is because one still has the counsel of prayer and plea.

This is the meaning of "My soul shall weep in secret," meaning when one comes to a state of concealment, then "My soul shall weep," because one has no other option.

Baal HaSulam, *Shamati [I Heard]*, Article no. 18,
"What Is My Soul Shall Weep In Secret"

Everything, great or small, is obtained only by the power of faith. And the reason why we must toil and labor is only to discover our lack of power and our lowliness—that we are unfit for anything by our own strength. And then we are ready to pour out a whole prayer before Him.

We could argue about that, "If this is so, then I will decide in advance that I am good for nothing, and why all the trouble and effort?" However, there is a law in nature that none is as wise as the experienced. Before a person actively tries to do all that is within his power, he is completely unfit to arrive at true lowliness, in the true measure mentioned above.

Hence, we must toil in Kedusha [holiness] and purity, as it is written, "Whatsoever you find that you can do by your own strength, do," and understand that for it is deep and true.

Even though you do not see a thing, since even when the required measure of labor has been made, this is the time for prayer, until then, believe in our sages, "I did not labor and found, do not believe." When the required measure is reached, your prayer will be whole and the Creator will respond generously, as our sages instructed us, "I labored and found, believe," for prior to that, you are unfit for prayer, and the Creator hears a prayer.

Baal HaSulam, Letter no. 57

The essence of the work is the choice, meaning "Therefore choose life," which is *Dvekut* [adhesion], which is *Lishma* [for Her name]. By that, one is rewarded with adhering to the Life of Lives.

When there is open Providence, there is no room for choice. Hence, the Upper One elevated *Malchut*, which is *Midat ha Din* [quality of judgment], to the *Eynaim* [eyes], which caused a concealment, meaning that the lower one sees that the Upper One is deficient, that there is no *Gadlut* [greatness] in the Upper One. At that time, the qualities of the Upper One are laid down in the lower one, meaning they are lacking. It follows that those *Kelim* have equality with the lower one: as there is no vitality in the lower one, there is no vitality in the Upper qualities, meaning that the Torah and *Mitzvot* are tasteless, lifeless.

And then there is room for choice, meaning that the lower one should say that all of this concealment that he feels is because the upper one restricted Himself for the sake of the lower one. This is called, "Israel that have been exiled, Divinity is with them," meaning he declares the flavor that he tastes, and it is not his fault that he feels no flavor of liveliness, but in his view, there truly is no vitality in the Upper One.

And if one overcomes and says that he finds a bitter taste in these nourishments only because he does not have the proper *Kelim* [vessels] to receive the abundance, as his *Kelim* are to receive and not to bestow, and regrets that the Upper One had to hide Himself, thus enabling the lower one to slander, this is considered that the lower one is raising MAN. By that, the Upper One raises His AHP—and ascent means that the Upper

One can show the lower one the praise and delight in the *Kelim* of *AHP*, which the Upper One can disclose. Thus, with respect to the lower one, it is found that he raises the *GE* of the lower one by the lower one himself seeing the merit of the Upper One. It follows that the lower one rises along with the *AHP* of the Upper One.

Rabash, *Steps of the Ladder,*
"Association of Mercy with Judgment"

One who was not rewarded with His love, it is as though all that he did in his work in the purity of the soul in the previous day has been completely burnt the following day. And each day and each moment he must begin anew, as though he had never done anything in his life. And then, "And the children of Israel sighed because of the work," since they evidently saw that they would never be able to produce anything from their own labor. For this reason, their sigh and prayer was whole, as it should be, and hence, "Their cry rose," etc., since the Creator hears a prayer, and only awaits a whole prayer.

Baal HaSulam, Letter no. 57

The labor and toil in one's heart during the prayer is the must reliable and most success-ful, and reaches its goal more than all other matters in reality.

Baal HaSulam, Letter no. 56

Anyone who comes to unify the Holy Name and did not intend in it in heart, and will, and fear, so the upper ones and lower ones will be blessed in him, his prayer is thrown outside.

The Book of Zohar with the *Sulam* [Ladder] Commentary, *BeShalach*, Item 278

Only the Light in the Torah Reforms the Person

Torah refers to the Light *clothed* in the Torah, meaning, as our sages said, "I have created the evil inclination, I have created the Torah as a spice." This refers to the Light in it, since the Light in it reforms it.

Baal HaSulam, *Shamati* [*I Heard*], Article no. 6,
"What Is Support in the Torah in the Work"

The Torah is the only spice to annul and subdue the evil inclination, as our sages said, "The Light in it reformed them."

Baal HaSulam, "The Teaching of the Kabbalah and Its Essence"

A person, born with the will to receive and wishing to correct it to in order to bestow, which is known to be against nature, has only one counsel: Only through the Light of the Torah can he invert into being in order to bestow.

Rabash, *The Rungs of the Ladder*,
"What Is Torah and Work on the Path of the Creator"

The most important thing is to be rewarded with *Dvekut* [adhesion] with the Creator, which is called "a vessel of bestowal," meaning equivalence of form. And this is why the remedy of Torah and *Mitzvot* was given, so that through it we will be able to exit self-love and reach love of others.

Rabash, *The Rungs of the Ladder*,
"What Is the Substance of Slander and Against Whom Is It?"

Our sages said, "I have created the evil inclination, I have created the Torah as a spice," meaning the Light spices the evil inclination. In other words, the Creator provides the strength to desire to do all of one's deeds for the sake of the Creator.

Rabash, *The Rungs of the Ladder*,
"As I am for Free, You Are for Free"

The Torah that we which engage in is in order to subdue the evil inclination, to attain *Dvekut* [adhesion] with the Creator: that all one's actions will be solely in order to bestow. Alone, it is impossible that one will able to go against nature, since the matter of mind and heart, in which one must be complemented, necessitates receiving assistance, and that assistance is through the Torah, as our sages said, "I have created the evil inclination, I have created the Torah as a spice." This is so because while engaging in It, the Light in it reforms them.

Rabash, *The Rungs of the Ladder*,
"What Is Torah and Work on the Path of the Creator"

Man was created with the will to receive self-pleasure, called "the will to receive for one's own benefit." We are told that one has to nullify that will to receive and acquire a new *Kli* [vessel], called "the will to bestow." Not every person is rewarded with it, meaning with the ability to acquire *Kelim* [vessels] suitable for the Upper Light to reside in.

For one to attain the will to bestow, our sages said (*Kiddushin* 30), "I have created the evil inclination, I have created for it the Torah as a spice," meaning that specifically through the Torah, one can achieve the *Kelim* of bestowal.

Rabash, *The Rungs of the Ladder*, "The Importance of Faith"

How one can achieve complete equivalence of form, so all one's actions are to give to others, while man's very essence is only to receive for oneself? By nature, we are unable to do even the smallest thing to benefit others...

Indeed, I admit that this is a very difficult thing. One cannot change the nature of one's own creation, which is only to receive for oneself, much less invert one's nature from one extreme to the other, meaning to not receive anything for oneself, but rather act only to bestow.

Yet, this is why the Creator gave us Torah and *Mitzvot*, which we were commanded to do only in order to bestow contentment upon the Creator. Had it not been for the engagement in Torah and *Mitzvot Lishma* (for Her Name), to bring contentment to the Creator with them, and not to benefit ourselves, there would have been no tactic in the world that could help us invert our nature.

Baal HaSulam, "A Speech for the Completion of The Zohar"

Through the natural remedy of the engagement in Torah and *Mitzvot Lishma*, which the Giver of the Torah knows, as our sages wrote (*Kidushin* 30b), "The Creator says, 'I have created the evil inclination, I have created for it the Torah as a spice.'" Thus, that creature develops and marches upward in degrees of the above spoken exaltedness, until he loses all remnants of self-love and all the *Mitzvot* in his body rise, and he performs all his actions only to bestow, so even the necessity that he receives flows in the direction of bestowal, so he can bestow.

Baal HaSulam, *Matan Torah* [The Giving of the Torah], Item 12

Thus, we see that the main work we must do, to achieve the purpose for which the world was created—to do good to His creations—is to *qualify ourselves to acquire vessels of bestowal*. This is the correction for making the King's gift complete, so they will feel no shame upon reception of the pleasures. And all the evil in us removes us from the good that we are destined to receive.

We were given the remedy of Torah and *Mitzvot* so as to achieve those *Kelim*. This is the meaning of what our sages said (*Kidushin*, 30), "The Creator says, 'I have created the evil inclination, I have created for it the spice of Torah,' by which he will lose all the sparks of self-love within him and will be rewarded with his desire being only to bestow contentment upon his Maker."

Rabash, *The Rungs of the Ladder*,
"What Is the Substance of Slander and Against Whom Is It?"

By not being able to exit the will to receive for oneself and feeling the need for the Creator's help, a need is born to be assisted by the Creator. The Creator's help is through the Torah, because the Light in it reforms him, meaning he receives vessels of bestowal.

Rabash, *The Rungs of the Ladder*,
"What Is the Foundation upon which Sanctity Is Built"

Our sages said, "The Creator said, 'I have created the evil inclination, I have created the Torah as a spice,'" meaning that the Torah and *Mitzvot* spice the evil inclination, to give it flavor, for the evil inclination is called the will to receive.

When it is for oneself, it is tasteless, for the restriction is over it, and it remains in a vacant space. But through Torah and *Mitzvot*, one reaches the intention to bestow, and with this vessel, called "will to receive," one receives all the delight and pleasure.

Rabash, *The Rungs of the Ladder*, "Concerning the Goal"

Our sages said, "I have created the evil inclination, I have created the Torah as a spice" (Babba Batra, 16). The matter of the spice is as our sages said, "If only they left Me and kept My Torah, the Light would reform them" (Yerushalmi, *Hagiga*, 6b). Thus, that there is a power in the Torah to reform a person, referring to the evil within man, meaning to make

241

the will to receive be in order to bestow.

Rabash, *The Rungs of the Ladder*, "Man Is Created in the Torah"

We see that the purpose of creating the worlds and the souls was entirely with one intention: to correct everything to be in order to bestow, which is called *Dvekut* [adhesion], "equivalence of form." The Creator said about the Torah, "I have created the evil inclination, I have created the spice." In other words, after a person receives the Torah as a spice, the evil inclination is corrected to being in order to bestow, as written in *The Zohar*, "The angel of death is to become a holy angel."

Rabash, *The Rungs of the Ladder*,
"What Is Torah and Work on the Path of the Creator"

Workers of the Creator Who Make the Torah Arid

Come and see the words of the sage, Rabbi Even Ezra in his book, *Yesod Mora*, p 8b: "And now note and know that all the *Mitzvot* that are written in the Torah or the conventions that the fathers have established, although they are mostly in action or in speech, they are all in order to correct the heart, 'for the Lord searches all hearts, and understands all the imaginations of the thoughts.'"

Baal HaSulam, "Introduction to the Book, Panim Meirot uMasbirot," Item 10

There is a common opinion that the prime goal of religion and the Torah is only the cleansing of actions, that all that is desired concerns observing the physical *Mitzvot* (commandments), without any additions or anything that should result from it. Had that been so, those who say that studying the revealed and practical actions alone is sufficient would be right.

Yet, this is not the case. Our sages have already said, "Why should the Creator mind if one slaughters at the throat or at the back of the neck? After all, the *Mitzvot* were only given to cleanse people." Thus, there is a purpose beyond the observance of the actions, and the actions are merely preparations for this purpose. Hence, clearly, if the actions are not arranged for the desired goal, it is as if nothing exists. And it is also written in *The Zohar*: "A *Mitzva* (commandment) without an aim is like a body without a soul." Hence, the aim, too, should accompany the act.

Baal HaSulam, "The Teaching of the Kabbalah and Its Essence"

A person, born with the will to receive and wishing to correct it to in order to bestow, which is known to be against nature, has only one counsel: Only through the Light of the Torah can he invert into being in order to bestow... Hence, such people who engage in Torah, not necessarily to know the laws and the customs, to know how to keep the *Mitzvot*, but who have another great role—to study Torah in order to correct the heart, these are called, "wise at heart." Everything is named after its action. Hence, Torah that is studied with this intention is called, "wise at heart," and not "wise in mind," since they need the Torah for the correction of the heart.

Rabash, *The Rungs of the Ladder*,
"What Is Torah and Work on the Path of the Creator"

The aridity and the darkness that have befallen us in this generation, such as we have never seen before. It is because even the worshipers of the Creator have abandoned the engagement in the secrets of the Torah.

So is the issue before us. If the worshipers of the Creator had, at least, engaged in the internality of the Torah and extended a complete Light from *Ein Sof*, the whole generation would have followed them. And everyone would be certain of their way, that they would not fall. But if even the servants of the Creator have distanced themselves from this wisdom, it is no wonder the whole generation is failing because of them. And because of my great sorrow I cannot elaborate on that!

Baal HaSulam, "Introduction to The Book of Zohar," Item 57

Those who engage solely in the dresses of the Torah are gravely mistaken, may God have mercy on them. And when the Creator's demand is abandoned and the majority of the multitude of the sages of the Torah do not know its purpose, and they consider the wisdom of the Torah with its purpose as mere addition of some quip to the laws—which, though truly sacred and precious—they will not illuminate our souls.

The Rav Raiah Kook, *Igrot* (Letters), Vol. 2, 153

This is the matter concerning the declining merit of the generations until they reached the final restriction in our generation, when the wisdom of writers is led astray and those who fear sin are despised. In that state, the masses are indifferent and working the Creator poses no obligation for them. Likewise, they feel no lack in its absence.

Even those engaging in the work, it is by rote. They are not thirsty, thriving to find some freshness of thought in their work. Were a sage to tell them, "Come let me I teach you wisdom, to understand and to teach the words of the Creator," one's immediate response would be, "In my heart, I already know that I will not be as Rashbi and his friends ... if I could only keep everything in its literal form." However, it is said about them, "The fathers ate sour grapes, and the children's teeth are blunted," for they engage in Torah and *Mitzvot* prematurely, and the teeth of their sons are made completely blunt, and they are surprised, "What is this work for you?" For you, and not for Him. And you, too, blunt his teeth. This is the form of our generation, which we are discussing.

Baal HaSulam, "The Remedy of Memory"

Woe unto them that make the spirit of Messiah leave and depart from the world, and cannot return to the world. They are the ones that make the Torah dry, without any moisture of comprehension and reason. They confine themselves to the practical part of the Torah, and do not wish to try to understand the wisdom of Kabbalah, to know and to understand the secrets of the Torah and the flavor of *Mitzva*. Woe unto them, for with these actions they bring about the existence of poverty, ruin, and robbery, looting, killing, and destructions in the world.

Baal HaSulam, "Introduction to The Book of Zohar," Item 70

Woe unto people from the affront of the Torah. For undoubtedly, when they engage only in the literal and in its stories, it wears its widow-garments, and covered with a bag. And all the nations shall say unto Israel: "What is thy Beloved more than another beloved? Why is your law more than our law? After all, your law, too, is stories of the mundane." There is no greater affront to the Torah than that. Hence, woe unto the people from the affront of the Torah. They do not engage in the wisdom of

Kabbalah, which honors the Torah, for they prolong the exile and all the afflictions that are about to come to the world.

The Writings of Ari, *The Tree of Life*, Part 1,
"Introduction of Chaim Vital," 11-12

The redemption of Israel and the rise of Israel depend on the study of *The Zohar* and the internality of the Torah. And vise versa, all the destruction and the decline of the Children of Israel are because they have abandoned the internality of the Torah. They have degraded its merit and made it seemingly redundant.

Baal HaSulam, "Introduction to The Book of Zohar," Item 69

The Creator gave us Torah and *Mitzvot*, which we were commanded to do only in order to bestow contentment upon the Creator. Had it not been for the engagement in Torah and *Mitzvot Lishma* (for Her Name), to bring contentment to the Creator with them, and not to benefit ourselves, there would have been no tactic in the world that could help us invert our nature.

Now you can understand the rigorousness of engaging in Torah and *Mitzvot Lishma*. If one's intention in the Torah and *Mitzvot* is not to benefit the Creator, but oneself, not only will the nature of the will to receive in him not be inverted, but rather, the will to receive in him will be much more than what he was given by the nature of his creation.

Baal HaSulam, "A Speech for the Completion of The Zohar"

But if a person from Israel degrades the virtue of the internality of the Torah and its secrets, which deals with the conduct of our souls and their degrees, and the perception and the tastes of the *Mitzvot* with regard to the advantage of the externality of the Torah, which deals only with the practical part? Also, even if one does occasionally engage in the internality of the Torah, and dedicates a little of one's time to it, when it is neither night nor day, as though it were redundant, by that one dishonors and degrades the internality of the world, which are the Children of Israel, and enhances the externality of the world – meaning the Nations of the World – over them. They will humiliate and disgrace the Children of Israel, and regard Israel as super-fluous, as though the world has no need for them, God forbid.

Furthermore, by that, they make even the externality in the Nations of the World overpower their own internality, for the worst among the Nations of the World, the harmful and the destructors of the world, rise above their internality, which are the Righteous of the Nations of the World. And then they make all the ruin and the heinous slaughter our generation had witnessed, may God pro-tect us from here on.

Baal HaSulam, "Introduction to The Book of Zohar," Item 69

Finally, I met with the famous ones among them, people who have already worn out their years delving in the writings of the Ari and *The Zohar*. They have so succeeded that they have become proficient and conversant in all the writings of the Ari.

They have a reputation as being the holiest people in the land. I asked them if they had studied with a Rav who attained the internality of the matters. They answered: "Heavens, no! There is no internality here whatsoever, but accurate texts, given to us, and nothing more than that, God forbid."

I asked them if Rav Chaim Vital had attained the internality of the matters. They replied: "He certainly did not attain more than we do." I then asked them about the Ari himself. I answered: "He certainly did not know the internality more than us at all, and all that he knew, he had passed on to his disciple, Rav Chaim Vital, and thus they came into our hands."

I mocked them: "How then were the matters composed in the heart of the Ari without any understanding and knowledge?" They replied: "He received the composition of these matters from Elijah, and he knew the internality, since he is an angel." Here my wrath poured out on them, for my patience to be with them had ended.

Baal HaSulam, "Introduction to the Book, From the Mouth of a Sage"

We learn from the words of the *Tikkunim* of *The Zohar* that there is an oath that the Light of Mercy and love will not awaken in the world before Israel's deeds in Torah and *Mitzvot* will have the intention to not receive reward, but only to bestow contentment upon the Maker. This is the meaning of the oath, "I adjure you, O daughters of Jerusalem."

Thus, the length of the exile and affliction that we suffer depends on us and waits for us to merit the practice of Torah and *Mitzvot Lishma*. And if we only attain that, this Light of love and Mercy, which has the power to extend, will immediately awaken, as it is written, "And the spirit shall rest upon him, the spirit of wisdom and understanding." Then we will be granted complete redemption.

Baal HaSulam, "Introduction to The Study of the Ten Sefirot," Item 36

THE APPROACH TO STUDYING THE WISDOM OF KABBALAH

The Remedy in the Engagement in the Wisdom of Kabbalah

Why did the Kabbalists obligate each person to study the wisdom of Kabbalah? Indeed, there is a great thing in it, worthy of being publicized: There is a wonderful, invaluable remedy to those who engage in the wisdom of Kabbalah. Although they do not understand what they are learning, through the yearning and the great desire to understand what they are learning, they awaken upon themselves the Lights that surround their souls.

Baal HaSulam, "Introduction to The Study of the Ten Sefirot," Item 155

We can learn the exalted matters called "the wisdom of Kabbalah" only through a *Segula* [power/remedy/virtue], as they can bring one a desire and urge to adhere to the Creator, due to the sanctity of the matters, which speak of the holy names. ...When one studies the exalted matters in order for them to bring him nearer to holiness, it results in drawing the Lights nearer. This means that this study will cause him to thus be rewarded with aiming all his actions to be in order to bestow. This is called "preparation work," for he prepares himself to be qualified to enter the King's and to cleave to the Creator.

Rabash, *The Rungs of the Ladder*, "Three Lines"

There is a magnificent power in it [In the Wisdom of Kabbalah]: All who engage in it, although they still do not understand what is written in it, are purified by it, and the Upper Lights draw closer to them.

Baal HaSulam, "The Teaching of the Kabbalah and Its Essence"

It is written *The Zohar*: "With this composition, the Children of Israel will be redeemed from exile." Also, in many other places, only through the expansion of the wisdom of Kabbalah in the masses will we obtain complete redemption.

They also said, "The Light in it reforms him." They were intentionally meticulous about it, to show us that only the Light enclosed within it, "like apples of gold in settings of silver," in it lies the cure that reforms a person. Both the individual and the nation will not complete the aim for which they were created, except by attaining the internality of the Torah and its secrets.

Baal HaSulam, "Introduction to the Book,
Panim Meirot uMasbirot," Item 5

Even when he does not have the vessels, when he engages in this wisdom, mentioning the names of the Lights and the vessels related to his soul, they immediately shine upon him to

a certain extent. However, they shine for him
without clothing the interior of his soul, for
lack of able vessels to receive them. Yet, the
illumination one receives time after time during the engagement draws upon him grace
from Above, imparting him with abundance
of sanctity and purity, which bring him much
closer to achieving perfection.

Baal HaSulam, "Introduction to The Study
of the Ten Sefirot," Item 155

There is a remedy in the Torah to reform a
person. This refers to the evil within a person, meaning that the will to receive will be
in order to bestow.

Rabash, *The Rungs of the Ladder*,
"As I am for Free, You Are for Free"

The Importance of
the Preparation for the Study

Prior to studying, one should focus on the
reason for which is he now studying Torah.

This is because every act must have some purpose, which is the cause for which he is not doing the deed. It is as our sages said, "A Prayer without intention is like a body without a soul." Hence, prior to studying the Torah, one should prepare the intention.

Rabash, *Steps of the Ladder*, "Man Is Created in the Torah"

Hence, the student pledges, prior to the study, to strengthen himself in faith in the Creator and in His guidance in reward and punishment, as our sages said, "Your landlord is liable to reward you for your work." One should aim one's labor to be for the *Mitzvot* of the Torah, and in this way, he will be imparted the pleasure of the Light in it. His faith will strengthen and grow through the remedy in this Light, as it is written, "It shall be health to thy navel, and marrow to thy bones" (Proverbs 3:8).

Then one's heart shall rest assured that from *Lo Lishma* he will come to *Lishma*. Thus, even one who knows about himself that he has not been rewarded with faith, still has hope through the practice of Torah.

For if one sets one's heart and mind to attain faith in the Creator through it, there is no greater *Mitzva* than that.

Baal HaSulam, "Introduction to The Study of the Ten Sefirot," Item 17

One should try to make a great effort, prior to studying, that his study will bear fruit and good results, meaning that the study will bring him the Light of Torah, by which it will be possible to reform him. Then, through the Torah, he becomes a wise disciple. What is a wise disciple? Baal HaSulam said, "One who learns from the Wise." The Creator is called "Wise," and one who learns from Him is called "a disciple of the Wise."

Rabash, *The Rungs of the Ladder*, "What Is Torah and Work on the Path of the Creator"

The goal of studying Torah is to attain feeling the Giver of the Torah. If a person does not place that goal before him, to attain the Giver of the Torah, he is considered "a gentile," meaning one who has no need for faith, a need to seek advice on how to obtain faith. Hence, he is still considered a gentile rather than Israel.

Rabash, *The Rungs of the Ladder*,
"What Is Torah and Work on the Path of the Creator"

The Importance of the Intention during the Study

The purpose of the study of Torah is to come to feel the Giver of the Torah.

Rabash, *The Rungs of the Ladder*,
"What Is Torah and Work on the Path of the Creator"

During the practice of Torah, every person must labor in it, and set his mind and heart to find "the light of the king's countenance" in it, that is, the attainment of open Providence, called "light of countenance." And any person is fit for it, as it is written, "those that seek Me shall find Me." ...Thus, one needs nothing in this matter except the labor alone.

Baal HaSulam, "Introduction to The Study
of the Ten Sefirot," Item 97

There is a wonderful, invaluable remedy to those who engage in the wisdom of Kabbalah. Although they do not understand what they are learning, through the yearning and the great desire to understand what they are learning, they awaken upon themselves the Lights that surround their souls.

Baal HaSulam, "Introduction to The Study
of the Ten Sefirot," Item 155

If he intends, while engaging in Torah, to study in order to receive the reward of the Torah, called "Light," then the study of Torah is beneficial. However, when he distracts his mind from the goal of studying Torah, the Torah is not instrumental in completing the work of making a vessel of bestowal

...This means that the force of Torah that should have subdued the evil inclination is cancelled. This is the meaning of the words, "Any Torah without work," meaning when he is not aiming for the Torah to do the work of inverting the vessels of reception to be in order to bestow, "Ends in annulment," meaning that that force is annulled.

Rabash, *The Rungs of the Ladder*,
"What Is Torah and Work on the Path of the Creator"

The Creator, who created it and gave the evil inclination its strength, evidently knew to create the remedy and the spice liable to wear off the power of the evil inclination and eradicate it altogether.

And if one practices Torah and fails to remove the evil inclination from himself, it is either that he has been negligent in giving the necessary labor and exertion in the practice of Torah, as it is written, "I have not labored but found, do not believe," or perhaps one did put in the necessary amount of labor, but has been negligent in the quality.

This means that while practicing Torah, they did not set their minds and hearts to draw the Light in the Torah, which brings faith to one's heart. Rather, they have been absent-minded about the principal require-ment demanded of the Torah, namely the Light that yields faith. And although they initially aimed for it, their minds went astray during the study.

Baal HaSulam, "Introduction to The Study of the Ten Sefirot," Item 18

One of the wonders of studying the secrets of Torah is that when a person studies these exalt-ed matters out of love and inner feeling, even though he is not capable of perceiving the mat-ters with clear, intellectual comprehension, they elevate his essence nonetheless, hence these matters shine their light upon him.

Rav Raiah Kook, *Orot HaTorah* [*Lights of the Torah*], Chapter 10, section 10

When one studies the exalted matters in order for them to bring him nearer to holiness, it results in drawing the Lights nearer. This means that this study will cause him to thus be rewarded with aiming all his actions to be in order to bestow. This is called "preparation work," for he prepares himself to be qualified to enter the King's and to cleave to the Creator.

Rabash, *The Rungs of the Ladder*, "Three Lines"

And when you aim—with humbleness and fear—to awaken the surrounding and the *Mochin*, although you do not know any essence, neither the surrounding and the *Mochin* nor anything else....Still, by your knowing, you evoke their existence. Although you do not know their essence, you draw great Light, and you serve the Creator with joy and true goodness of heart, as a result of the greatness of the Light shining upon you.

Rav Yitzhak Yehuda Yehiel Safrin of Komarno, *Netiv HaYichud* [Path of Unification]

It is written: "And you studied It day and night," and it does not say: "And you understood It day and night." If you understand-you understand, and if not-the reward of studying is in your hand. Evidence is found in *The Book of Zohar*, for although one does not understand, the language remedies the soul.

The Ramchal, 138, *Pitchei Hochmah [Doors to Wisdom]*, Introduction

A person, born with the will to receive and wishing to correct it to in order to bestow, which is known to be against nature, has only one counsel: Only through the Light of the Torah can he invert into being in order to bestow... Hence, such people who engage in Torah, not necessarily to know the laws and the customs, to know how to keep the *Mitzvot*, but who have another great role—to study Torah in order to correct the heart, these are called, "wise at heart." Everything is named after its action. Hence, Torah that is studied with this intention is called, "wise at heart,"

and not "wise in mind," since they need the
Torah for the correction of the heart.

Rabash, *The Rungs of the Ladder*,
"What Is Torah and Work on the Path of the Creator"

One who studies Torah in order to know resembles someone studying a diary, that surely
would not help in studying, and no benefit
would come to him as a result, hopefully he
would not lose either. However, when one
approaches the study of Torah, his intention
should be that he is thereby studying that
matter for their Divine words, their intensity
of internality is concealed. Thus, the sense-
lessness he speaks of Torah will be improved
before the Lord.

Ramak, *Know the God of your Father*, 59

FROM LOVE OF OTHERS
TO LOVE OF THE CREATOR

Love of Others Is the Means to Attain the Love of the Creator

The first stage is love between friends and then they can attain the love of the Creator.

Rabash, *The Rungs of the Ladder*,
"What Is the Substance of Slander and Against Whom Is It?"

Bear in mind that the Mitzvot between man and man come before the Mitzvot between man and God, because the bestowal upon one's friend brings one to bestow upon his Maker.

Baal HaSulam, "Introduction to The Book of Zohar," Item 19

We must understand the essence of the love of God from the properties of love by which one person relates to another. The love of

God is necessarily given through these qualities, since they were only imprinted in humans for His name to begin with.

Baal HaSulam, "Introduction to The Study of the Ten Sefirot," Item 69

When one completes one's work in love and bestowal for one's fellow person and comes to the highest point, one also completes one's love and bestowal for the Creator. In that state there is no difference between the two, for anything that is outside one's body, meaning one's self-interest is judged equally - either to bestow upon one's friend or bestow contentment upon one's Maker.

Baal HaSulam, "The Love for the Creator & Love for the Created Beings"

The impression that comes to a person when engaging in *Mitzvot* between man and God is completely the same as the impression he gets when engaging in *Mitzvot* between man and man. He is obliged to perform all the *Mitzvot*

Lishma (for Her name), without any hope for self-love, meaning that no light or hope returns to him through his trouble in the form of reward or honor, etc. Here, in this exalted point, the love of the Creator and the love of his friend unite and actually become one.

Baal HaSulam, The *Arvut* [Mutual Guarantee], Item 22

There are two parts to the Torah: one concerns man and God; the other concerns man and man. And I call upon you to, at any rate, engage and assume that which concerns man and man, since thus you will also learn the part that concerns man and God.

Baal HaSulam, "One Commandment"

Even if we see that there are two parts to the Torah: The first—*Mitzvot* between man and God, and the second - *Mitzvot* between man and man, they are both one and the same thing. This means that the actual purpose of them and the desired goal are one, namely *Lishma*.

It makes no difference if one works for one's friend or for the Creator. That is because it is carved in us by the nature of creation that anything that comes from the outside appears empty and unreal.

Baal HaSulam,
"The Love for the Creator & Love for the Created Beings"

This is what Hillel Hanasi assumed, that "Love thy friend as thyself" is the ultimate goal in the practice. That is because it is the clearest form to mankind.

We should not be mistaken with deeds, for they are set before ones eyes. We know that if we place the needs of our friends before our own, it is bestowal. For that reason Hillel does not define the goal as "And you shall love the Lord your God with all your heart and with all your soul and with all your might," because they are indeed one and the same thing. It is so because one should also love one's friend with all his heart and with all his soul and with all his might, because that is the meaning of the words "as thyself." After all one certainly loves oneself with all one's heart and soul and might, but with regards to the Creator, one may deceive oneself; and with one's friend it is always spread out before his eyes.

Baal HaSulam,
"The Love for the Creator & Love for the Created Beings"

We should know that there is a virtue to love of friends: one cannot deceive himself and say that he loves the friends if in fact he doesn't love them. Here he can examine whether he truly has love of friends or not. But with love of the Creator, one cannot examine oneself, if his intention is the love of the Creator, meaning that he wants to bestow upon the Creator, or his desire is to receive in order to receive.

Rabash, *Rabash—the Social Writings*, "Come unto Pharaoh (2)"

The part of the Torah that deals with man's relationship with his friend is more capable of bringing one to the desired goal. This is because the work in *Mitzvot* between man and God is fixed and specific, and is not demanding, and one becomes easily accustomed to it, and everything that is done out of habit is no longer useful. But the *Mitzvot* between man and man are changing and irregular, and demands surround him wherever he may turn. Hence, their cure is much more certain and their aim is closer.

Baal HaSulam, *Matan Torah* [The Giving of the Torah], Item 14

With respect to a person who is still within the nature of Creation, there is no difference between the love of God and the love of his fellow person.

This is because anything that is not him is unreal to him. And because that proselyte asked of Hillel Hanasi to explain to him the desired outcome of the Torah, so his goal would be near, and he would not have to walk a long way, as he said, "Teach me the whole Torah while I am standing on one leg;" hence, he defined it for him as love of his friend because its aim is nearer and is revealed faster, since it is mistake-proof and is demanding.

Baal HaSulam, *Matan Torah* [The Giving of the Torah], Item 15

He who thinks that he is deceiving his friend, is really deceiving the Creator, since besides man's body there is only the Creator. This is because it is the essence of creation that man is called "creature" only with respect to himself. The Creator wants man to feel that he is a separated reality from Him; but except for that, it is all "the whole earth is full of His glory."

Hence, when lying to one's friend, one is lying to the Creator; and when saddening one's friend, one is saddening the Creator. For this reason, if one is accustomed to speak the truth, it will help him with respect to the Creator.

Baal HaSulam, *Shamati* [I Heard], Article no. 67, "Depart from Evil"

There are two parts in the Torah: 1) *Mitzvot* between man and God, and 2) *Mitzvot* between man and man. And they both aim for the same thing – to bring the creature to the final purpose of *Dvekut* with Him.

Furthermore, even the practical side in both of them is really one and the same, because when one performs an act *Lishma*, without any mixture of self-love, meaning without finding any benefit for himself, then one does not feel any difference whether one is working to love one's friend or to love the Creator.

Baal HaSulam, *Matan Torah* [The Giving of the Torah], Item 13

There is no other cure for humanity but the acceptance of the commandment of Providence: bestowal upon others in order to bring contentment to the Creator in the measure of the two verses.

The first is "love thy friend as thyself," which is the attribute of the work itself. This means that the measure of work to bestow upon others for the happiness of society should be no less than the measure imprinted in man to care for his own needs. Moreover, he should put his fellow person's needs before his own.

And the other verse is, "And you shall love the Lord thy God with all thy heart, and with all thy soul, and with all thy might." This is the goal that must be before everyone's eyes when laboring for one's friend's needs. This means that he labors and toils only to be liked by the Creator.

Baal HaSulam, "The Peace"

A Prayer of Many

When one evokes self-pity, he is engaged in receiving for himself. The more he prays, not only does he not prepare a vessel of equivalence, on the contrary, sparks of reception are thus nurtured in him. It follows that he is going the opposite way, meaning he should prepare a vessel of bestowal, but he has prepared a vessel of reception.

Thus, when he prays for the collective, by that prayer, he engages in bestowal. And the more he prays, to that extent he molds a vessel for bestowal, upon which the Light of bestowal, called "merciful," can be revealed.

And by receiving the Light of mercy, the quality of "compassionate" can be revealed. ...This means that by having received the Light of mercy, he is qualified to receive the Light of love.

Rabash, *Steps of the Ladder*, "Flee, My Beloved"

One should not ask the Creator to draw him near Him, since that is insolent of the person, for in what way is he more important than others? Whereas when he prays for the society—which is *Malchut*, called "the assembly of Israel", the entirety of the souls—that Divinity is in the dust, and prays for Her to ascend, meaning that the Creator will illuminate the darkness within her, then the whole of Israel will ascend in degrees, including the entreating individual, for he is part of the society as well.

Rabash, *Steps of the Ladder*, "The Ruin of Sanctity"

That worker of the Creator who does not feel the sorrow of the public, but feels only his own lack, his receptacle for receiving abundance is no larger, too. For this reason, he will not be able to receive the general revelation of Divinity as the consolation of the public, since he has not prepared a receptacle from this general aspect, but only his individual aspect.

But one who feels the sorrow of the public and senses the society's distress as his own personal distress is rewarded with seeing the complete revelation of Divinity, meaning the consolations of the whole of Israel, for his lack is a general lack. Hence, the Divine

Abundance is general as well.

Baal HaSulam, *A Sages Fruit*, Vol. 3,
"All Who Feel the Sorrow of the Public"

It is a prevailing law that man himself is called "a creature," meaning he alone. Other than him it is already the Holy Divinity. It follows that when he is praying for his contemporaries, it is considered that he is praying for the Holy Divinity, who is in exile and in need of all the salvations. That is the meaning of eternality, and particularly so can the Light of Mercy be revealed.

Rabash, *Steps of the Ladder*, "Flee, My Beloved"

"He hears the prayer." The world asks why "prayer" is in the singular form, since the Creator hears prayers, as it is written, "For You hear the prayer of every mouth of Your people, Israel, with mercy." It should be interpreted that there is only one prayer we need not pray—to raise Divinity from the dust, by which all salvation will take place.

Rabash, *Steps of the Ladder*, "He Hears the Prayer"

Our sages said, "Anyone who is saddened for the public is rewarded and sees the comfort of the public." The public is called "The Holy *Shechina* (Divinity)," since public means a collective, meaning the assembly of Israel, since *Malchut* is the collection of all the souls.

Baal HaSulam, *Shamati* [*I Heard*], Article no. 35, "Concerning the Vitality of Kedusha"

The Nature of Man and the Nature of the Creator

Man's Essence Is the Will to Receive

The desire is the "self" of the person.

Baal HaSulam, *Shamati [I Heard]*, Article no. 153,
"A Thought Is an Upshot of the Desire"

Our essence is as the essence of all the details in reality, which is no more and no less than the will to receive.

Baal HaSulam, "Introduction to The Book of Zohar," Item 20

The very essence of the soul is a will to receive. And the difference we can tell between one object and another is discerned only by its will.

Baal HaSulam, "Introduction to The Book of Zohar," Item 21

The primary innovation, from the perspective of Creation, which He has created existence from absence, applies to one aspect only, defined as the "will to receive."

Baal HaSulam, "The Freedom"

All the corporeal entities in our world, that is, everything within that space, be it still, vegetative, animate, a spiritual object or a corporeal object, if we want to distinguish the unique, self aspect of each of them, how they differentiate from one another, even in the smallest of particles, it amounts to no more than a "desire to receive."

Baal HaSulam, "The Freedom"

All the vessels and the bodies, both from spiritual worlds and from physical worlds, are deemed spiritual or corporeal substance, whose nature is the will to receive.

Baal HaSulam, "The Freedom"

Concerning the soul, which is a part of God above, the Kabbalists compared it to a rock carved from a mountain. The question arises, "How can it be said that it is the same substance as the mountain which is from His essence?" It should be interpreted that they are referring to existence from existence, hence they compared it to a rock from a mountain. The difference is in that it is part of the thing, a part which is to be called "soul." This is the will to receive, meaning that this part is called "Creation," meaning existence from absence.

Rabash, *Steps of the Ladder*, "The Substance of the Soul"

Creation refers to appearance of something that did not exist before. This is considered existence from absence. Yet, how do we picture something that is not included in Him, since He is almighty and includes all of them together? And also, one does not give what is not in Him.

As we have said, the whole Creation that He created is only the *Kelim* (plural for *Kli*) of the souls, which is the will to receive. This is quite clear, since He necessarily does not have a will to receive, as from whom would He receive? Hence, this is truly a new Creation, not a trace of which existed previously, and is hence considered existence from absence.

Baal HaSulam,
"Introduction to the Preface to the Wisdom of Kabbalah," Item 4

Egoism Is Embedded in the Nature of Every Person

Egoism is embedded in the nature of every person, as in any animal.

Baal HaSulam, "The Solution"

Man was created with the nature of wanting to please only himself.

Rabash, *Steps of the Ladder*,
"One Studies Only where One's Heart Desires"

One cannot make a single movement without any benefit for oneself.

Baal HaSulam, "A Speech for the Completion of The Zohar"

"A wild ass shall be turned into man" (Job 11:12), because when one emerges out of the bosom of Creation, one is in utter filth and lowliness, meaning a multitude of self-love that is imprinted in him, whose every movement revolves solely around himself, without a shred of bestowal upon others.

Baal HaSulam, *Matan Torah* [The Giving of the Torah], Item 12

While man's very essence is only to receive for oneself. By nature, we are unable to do even the smallest thing to benefit others. Instead, when we give to others, we are compelled to expect that in the end, we will receive a worthwhile reward.

Baal HaSulam, "A Speech for the Completion of The Zohar"

The equal side in all the people of the world is that each of us stands ready to abuse and exploit all the people for his own private benefit with every means possible, without taking into any consideration that he is going to build himself on the ruin of his friend.

Baal HaSulam, "Peace in the World"

The nature of each and every person is to exploit the lives of all other people in the world for his own benefit. And all that he gives to another is only out of necessity; and even then there is exploitation of others in it, but it is done cunningly, so that his friend will not notice it and concede willingly.

Baal HaSulam, "Peace in the World"

It is a natural law for any being, that anything outside one's own body is regarded as unreal and empty. And any movement that a person makes to love another is performed with a Reflected Light, and some reward that will eventually return to him and serve him for his own good. Thus, such an act cannot be considered "love of another" because it is judged by its end. It is like rent that finally pays off. However, the act of renting is not considered love of another.

But making any kind of movement only as a result of love for others, without any spark of Reflected Light, and no hope for any kind of self-gratification in return, is completely impossible by nature.

Baal HaSulam, *Matan Torah* [The Giving of the Torah], Item 13

Regarding the term "egoism," I am not referring to the original egoism. Rather I am referring primarily to the narrow egoism. This is because the original egoism is only self-love, which is its entire positive, individual force of existence. In that respect, it does not altogether contradict the altruistic force, although it does not serve it.

However, it is in the nature of egoism that as it is used, it becomes extremely narrow, for it is more or less obliged to take on the nature of hatred and exploitation of others, in order to ease one's own existence. That does not refer to abstract hatred, rather to what is revealed in acts of exploitation of one's friend for one's own benefit, becoming increasingly foul according to its degrees, such as cunningness, theft, robbery, and murder. This is called "narrow egoism," and in that respect it contradicts and is the complete opposite of the love of others. This is the negative force that destroys the society.

Baal HaSulam, "The Nation"

The Superiority of Man to the Beast

We find that the only need in man's wishes, which does not exist in the whole of the animate species, is the awakening towards Godly *Dvekut* (adhesion). Only the human species is ready for it, and none other.

It follows that the whole issue of presence in the human species is in that preparation imprinted in him to crave His work, and in that, he is superior to the beast.

Baal HaSulam, "This Is for Judah"

The absence that precedes man's existence is the form of the beast. This is why it is written, "a wild ass's colt is born a man," as it is necessary for every person to begin in the state of a beast. And the writing says, "Man and beast Thou preserves, O Lord." And as a beast is given all that it needs for its sustenance and the fulfillment of its purpose, He also provides man with all that is necessary for his substance and the fulfillment of his purpose.

Therefore, we should understand where is the advantage of man's form over the beast, from the perspective of their own preparation. Indeed, it is discerned in their wishes, since man's wishes are certainly different from those of a beast. And to that extent, God's salvation of man differs from God's salvation of a beast.

Baal HaSulam, "This Is for Judah"

All animals completely rely on nature and are utterly incapable of progressing beyond nature, helping themselves without it.

Man, however, has been gifted with the power of thought. Using this power, he gradually becomes free of the chains of nature and surpasses it. He imitates the work of nature and works similarly. He does not wait for nature to give him chicks, for the hen to come and incubate the eggs. Instead, he builds a machine that incubates the eggs and hatches chicks for him, just as the natural hen.

Baal HaSulam, "The Nation"

And the most important thing in this whole diverse reality is the sensation given to the animals—that each of them feels its own existence. And the most important sensation is the noetic sensation, given to man alone, by which one also feels what is in one's other—the pains and comforts. Hence, it is certain that if the Creator has a purpose in this Creation, its subject is man. It is said about him, "All of the Lord's works are for him."

Baal HaSulam, "The Teaching of the Kabbalah and Its Essence"

The spirit of the beast descends, meaning it sees only from itself onward. It does not have the intellect and wisdom to look at the past in order to correct the future. Man has an advantage to it for the spirit of man rises, meaning toward the past, looking at the past as one looks in the mirror to see how to correct one's flaws. Similarly, the mind views past experiences and mends one's ways henceforth.

This is why beasts do not evolve and they are still standing in the same place where they were created, since they do not have the mirror through which to understand how to correct the ways and gradually develop, as does man. Man evolves daily until his superiority is assured and sensed, for he is yet to ride upon the high planets.

Baal HaSulam, "Writings of the Last Generation"

And now sons do hear me: The "Wisdom cries aloud in the streets, she utters her voice," "Whoso is on the Lord's side, let him come unto me," "For it is no vain thing for you; because it is your life, and the length of your days."

"You were not created to follow the act of the grain and the potato, you and your asses in one trough." And as the purpose of the ass is not to serve all its contemporary asses, man's purpose is not to serve all the bodies of the people of his time, the contemporaries of his physical body. Rather, the purpose of the ass is to serve and be of use to man, who is superior to it, and the purpose of man is to serve the Creator and complete His aim.

Baal HaSulam, "Introduction to the Book, Panim Meirot uMasbirot," Item 6

Animate: We see that each animal has its own characteristic; they are not confined to the environment but each of them has its own sensation and characteristic. They can certainly operate against the will of the

Landlord, meaning they can work in bestowal and are also not confined to the environment. Rather, they have their own lives, and their vitality does not depend on their friends' life. Yet, they cannot feel more than their own being. In other words, they have no sensation of the other. And naturally cannot care for the other.

Speaking has virtues: 1) It acts against the will of the Landlord. 2) It is not confined to its contemporaries like the vegetative, meaning it is independent from the environment. 3) It also feels the other, and hence can care for them and complement them, by feeling and regretting with the public, and being able to rejoice in the solace of the public, and by the ability to receive from the past and from the future. Animals, however, feel only the present and only their own being.

Baal HaSulam, *Shamati [I Heard]*, Article no. 115,

"Still, Vegetative, Animate, and Speaking"

Concerning Still, Vegetative, Animal and Speaking:

Man's advantage over animals is that he can aim at a remote goal, meaning to agree to a certain amount of current pain, out of choice of future benefit or pleasure, to be attained after some time.

Baal HaSulam, "The Freedom"

And man's pre-eminence over all animals is that our minds are developed to such an extent that all the body's events are depicted in our brains as images that we experience as concepts and rationalities.

Thus, the mind and all its deductions are but products that extend from the events of the body.

Baal HaSulam, "Body and Soul"

The Animate. Each creature feels itself, concerning attracting what is beneficial to it and rejecting the harmful. It follows that one animal equalizes in value to all the plants in reality. It is so because the force that distinguishes the beneficial from the detrimental in the entire Vegetative is found in one creature in the Animate, separated to its own authority.

This sensing force in the Animate is very limited in time and space, since the sensation does not operate at even the shortest distance outside its body. Also, it does not feel anything outside its own time, meaning in the past or in the future, but only at the present moment.

Atop them is the Speaking, consisting of an emotional force and an intellectual force together. For this reason, its power is unlimited by time and space in attracting what is good for it and rejecting what is harmful, like the Animate.

This is so because of its science, which is a spiritual matter, unlimited by time and place. One can teach others wherever they are in the whole of reality, and in the past and the future throughout the generations.

Baal HaSulam, "Introduction to the Book,
Panim Meirot uMasbirot," Item 3

The Subject of the Purpose of Creation Is Man

Everything is for man.

The Book of Zohar with the *Sulam* [Ladder] commentary,
Toldot, Item 2

The value of one person from the Speaking equalizes with the value of all the forces in the Vegetative and the Animate in the whole of reality at that time, and in all the past generations. This is so because its power encompasses them and contains them within its own self, along with all their forces.

Baal HaSulam, "Introduction to the Book,
Panim Meirot uMasbirot," Item 3

And we must not ponder the state of other beings in the world but man, since man is the center of Creation. And all other creatures do not have any value of their own but to the extent that they help man achieve his perfection. Hence, they rise and fall with him without any consideration of themselves.

Baal HaSulam,
"Introduction to The Book of Zohar," Item 18

And the most important thing in this whole diverse reality is the sensation given to the animals—that each of them feels its own existence. And the most important sensation is the noetic sensation, given to man alone, by which one also feels what is in one's other— the pains and comforts. Hence, it is certain that if the Creator has a purpose in this Creation, its subject is man. It is said about him, "All of the Lord's works are for him."

Baal HaSulam,
"The Teaching of the Kabbalah and Its Essence"

This purpose of Creation does not apply to the still and the great spheres, such as the earth, the moon, or the sun, however luminous they may be, and not to the vegetative or the animate, for they lack the sensation of others, even from among their own species. Therefore, how can the sensation of the Godly and His bestowal apply to them?

Humankind alone, having been prepared with the sensation of others of the same species, who are similar to them, after delving in Torah and *Mitzvot*, when they invert their will to receive to a will to bestow, and come to equivalence of form with his Maker, they receive all the degrees that have been prepared for them in the Upper Worlds, called *NRN-HY*. By that they become qualified to receive the purpose of the Thought of Creation. After all, the purpose of the creation of all the worlds was for man alone.

Baal HaSulam, "Introduction to The Book of Zohar," Item 39

The Discrepancy between Man's Nature and the Nature of the Creator

"A wild ass shall be turned into man" (Job 11:12), because when one emerges out of the bosom of Creation, one is in utter filth and lowliness, meaning a multitude of self-love that is imprinted in him, whose every movement revolves solely around himself, without a shred of bestowal upon others.

Thus, then one is at the farthest distance from the root, on the other end, since the root is all bestowal without a hint of reception, whereas the newborn is in a state of complete self-reception without a hint of bestowal. Therefore, his situation is regarded as being at the lowest point of lowliness and filth in our human world.

Baal HaSulam, *Matan Torah* [The Giving of the Torah], Item 12

Although the will to receive is a mandatory law in the creature, as it is the essence of the creature and the proper *Kli* [vessel] for reception of the goal of the Thought of Creation, it nonetheless completely separates it from the Emanator. This is so because there is disparity of form to the point of oppositeness between itself and the Emanator, as the Emanator is complete bestowal without a shred of reception, and the creature is complete reception without a shred of bestowal. Thus, there is no greater oppositeness of form than that. It therefore follows that this oppositeness of form necessarily separates it from the Emanator.

Baal HaSulam, "Preface to the Wisdom of Kabbalah," Item 13

Evil, in general, is nothing more than self-love, called "egoism," since it is opposite in form from the Creator, who hasn't any will to receive for Himself, but only to bestow.

Baal HaSulam, "The Essence of Religion and Its Purpose"

Remoteness from the Creator Is the Reason for all Suffering

The Light of the King's Face is surely life, and its concealment is the source of all evil.

Ramchal, *Daat Tevunot (Knowledge of Intelligence)*, 40

The reason for our great distance from the Creator, and that we are so prone to transgress His will, is for but one reason, which became the source of all the torment and the suffering that we suffer, and for all the sins and the mistakes that we fail in. Clearly, by removing that reason, we will instantly be rid of any sorrow and pain. We will immediately be granted adhesion with Him in heart, soul, and might. And I tell you that that preliminary reason is none other than the "lack of our understanding in His Providence over His creations," that we do not understand Him properly.

Baal HaSulam, "Introduction to The Study of the Ten Sefirot," Item 42

All entanglement of people's views and all the internal contradictions that each individual suffers in his views stem only from the obscurity of thought regarding the Godly concept.

Rav Raiah Kook, *Orot [Lights]*, 124

Evil, in general, is nothing more than self-love, called "egoism," since it is opposite in form from the Creator, who hasn't any will to receive for Himself, but only to bestow.

Baal HaSulam, "The Essence of Religion and Its Purpose"

And although we have clarified (about the quality of uniqueness) that it comes from a sublime reason, that this attribute extends to us directly from the Creator, who is single in the world and the Root of all creations, still, out of the sensation of singularity, when it sits within our narrow egoism, it affects ruin and destruction until it became the source of all the ruins that were and will be in the world.

Baal HaSulam, "Peace in the World"

Pleasure and sublimity are measured by the extent of equivalence of form with the Maker. And pain and intolerance are measured by the extent of disparity of form from the Maker. Thus, egoism is loathsome and pains us, as its form is opposite from the Maker.

Baal HaSulam, "The Essence of Religion and Its Purpose"

Indeed, when all human beings agree to abolish and eradicate their will to receive for themselves, and have no other desire but to bestow upon their friends, all worries and jeopardy in the world would cease to exist. And we would all be assured of a whole and wholesome life, since each of us would have a whole world caring for us, ready to fulfill our needs.

Yet, while each of us has only a desire to receive for ourselves, it is the source of all the worries, suffering, wars, and slaughter we cannot escape. They weaken our bodies with all sorts of sores and maladies.

Baal HaSulam, "Introduction to The Book of Zohar," Item 19

But if ... a person from Israel degrades the virtue of the internality of the Torah and its secrets, which deals with the conduct of our souls and their degrees, and the perception and the tastes of the *Mitzvot* with regard to the advantage of the externality of the Torah, which deals only with the practical part? Also, even if one does occasionally engage in the internality of the Torah, and dedicates a little of one's time to it, when it is neither night nor day, as though it were redundant, by that one dishonors and degrades the internality of the world, which are the Children of Israel, and enhances the externality of the world – meaning the Nations of the World – over them. They will humiliate and disgrace the Children of Israel, and regard Israel as superfluous, as though the world has no need for them, God forbid.

Furthermore, by that, they make even the externality in the Nations of the World overpower their own internality, for the worst among the Nations of the World, the harmful and the destructors of the world, rise above their internality, which are the Righteous of the Nations of the World. And then they make all the ruin and the heinous slaughter our generation had witnessed, may God protect us from here on.

Baal HaSulam, "Introduction to The Book of Zohar," Item 69

We learn from the words of the *Tikkunim* of *The Zohar* that there is an oath that the Light of Mercy and love will not awaken in the world before Israel's deeds in Torah and *Mitzvot* will have the intention to not receive reward, but only to bestow contentment upon the Maker. This is the meaning of the oath, "I adjure you, O daughters of Jerusalem."

Thus, the length of the exile and affliction that we suffer depends on us and waits for us to merit the practice of Torah and *Mitzvot Lishma*. And if we only attain that, this Light of love and Mercy, which has the power to extend, will immediately awaken, as it is written, "And the spirit shall rest upon him, the spirit of wisdom and understanding." Then we will be granted complete redemption.

Baal HaSulam, "Introduction to The Study of the Ten Sefirot," Item 36

Two Ways to Discover the Wholeness

There are two ways to discover the completeness: the path of Torah and the path of pain.

Baal HaSulam, "The Solution"

There are two authorities here, acting in the conduct of development: the one is the authority of Heaven, which is sure to turn anything harmful and evil to good and useful, but that will be in due time, in its own way, in a floundering manner and after a long time. And then there is the authority of the earth. And when the "evolving object" is a living being, it suffers horrendous torments while under the "press of development," a press that carves its way ruthlessly.

The "authority of the earth," however, is comprised of people who have taken the laws of development under their own government and can free themselves entirely from the chains of time, and who greatly accelerate time, the completion of the ripeness and correction of the object, which is the end of its development.

Baal HaSulam, "Peace in the World"

Bear in mind that two forces serve to push us up the rungs of the aforementioned ladder, until we reach its head in the sky, which is the purposeful point of equivalence of form with our Maker. And the difference between these two forces is that the first pushes us from behind, which we defined as "the path of pain" or "the way of the earth."

...The second force pushes us consciously, that is, of our own choice. That force pulls us from before, and that is what we defined as "the path of Torah and *Mitzvot*." For observing Torah and *Mitzvot* in order to bring contentment to our Maker rapidly develops that sense of recognition of evil, as we have shown in *Matan Torah* [The Giving of the Torah] (Item 13).

And here we benefit twice:

A. We do not have to wait for life's ordeals to push us from behind, whose measure of goading is gauged only by the measure of agony and destructions. On the contrary, through the subtle pleasantness we feel when working sincerely to Him, to please Him, there develops within us a relative recognition of the lowliness of these sparks of self-love—that they are obstacles on our way to receiving that subtle taste of bestowal upon the Creator. Thus, the gradual sense of recognition of evil evolves in us from times of delight and great tranquility, through reception of the good while serving the Creator, out of our sensation of the pleasantness and gentleness that reach us due to the equivalence of form with our Maker.

B. We save time, for He operates to "enlighten" us, thus enabling us to increase our work and hasten time as we please.

Baal HaSulam, "The Essence of Religion and Its Purpose"

It is true that people could be rewarded with their deeds, realize the truth, and leave the lying ways of this world, in their desire to draw near to their Creator. That is as they already know and understand that everything opposite from the path the Creator commanded is only the evil kind that the Upper Will desired and created while concealing the face of His benevolence.

Hence, they will loathe this deception of their eyes and will choose the hidden and concealed Light—the Light of the face of the King if the living. And if they would do so,

His uniqueness would be revealed to them by themselves and they would be drawing salvation toward themselves. There would be no need for the Creator to show Himself to them through the hardship and length of the exile, for since the truth would be clarified to them of their own minds, that would suffice. And when it is clarified, it is clarified.

Since they had already seen the evil and recognized it, and have left it to hold the truth of His uniqueness, indeed, what needed to be done was done, as the intent is only that this matter would be verified for them, so that henceforth, they would delight in the truth that has been revealed to them. Thus, when it is revealed, it is revealed.

Ramchal, *Daat Tevunot* [*Knowledge of Intelligence*], 40

[The] law of development, which is spread over the whole of reality, is guaranteed to return all evil to good and useful acts through the power of the Government of Heaven

Above, meaning without asking permission from the people who inhabit the earth. However, the Creator placed knowledge and authority in the hands of man and permitted him to accept the above-mentioned law of development under his own authority and government, and handed him the ability to hasten the process of development as he wishes, freely and completely independent of the boundaries of time.

Baal HaSulam, "Peace in the World"

Now you can understand their words about the verse, "I, the Lord, will hasten it in its time." The *Sanhedrin* (98) interpreted, "Not rewarded—in its time; rewarded—I will hasten it."

Thus, there are two ways to attain the above-mentioned goal: through their own attention, which is called a "Path of Repentance." If they are awarded that, then "I will hasten it" will be applied to them. This means that there is no set time for it, but when they are awarded, the correction ends, of course.

If they are not awarded the attention, there is another way, called "Path of Suffering" ...that can cleanse any defect and materialism until one realizes how to raise one's head out of the beastly crib, to soar and climb the rungs of the ladder of happiness and human success, for one will cleave to one's root and complete the aim.

Baal HaSulam, "Introduction to the Book,
Panim Meirot uMasbirot," Item 7

Therefore, the end is certain to come to Israel by the law of gradual development, and it is called "in its time," meaning tied to the chains of time. And Israel's guaranteed end, by taking the development of their attributes under their own authority is called, "I will hasten it," meaning completely independent of time.

Baal HaSulam, "Peace in the World"

FREEDOM OF CHOICE

Does a Person Have Free Choice?

We are all like machines, operating and creating through external forces, which force them to act this way. This means that we are all incarcerated in the prison of Providence, which, using these two chains, pleasure and pain, pushes and pulls us to its will, to where it sees fit.

It turns out that there is no such thing as selfishness in the world, since no one here is free or stands on his own two feet. I am not the owner of the act, and I am not the performer because I want to perform, but I am performed upon, in a compulsory manner, and without my awareness.

Baal HaSulam, "The Freedom"

When we examine the acts of an individual, we shall find them compulsory. He is compelled to do them and has no freedom of choice. In a sense, he is like a stew cooking on a stove; it has no choice but to cook. And it must cook because Providence has harnessed life with two chains: pleasure and pain. ...And when all is said and done, there is no difference here between man and animal. And if that is the case, there is no free choice whatsoever, but a pulling force, drawing them toward any bypassing pleasure and rejecting them from painful circumstances. And Providence leads them to every place it chooses by means of these two forces, without asking their opinion in the matter.

Moreover, even determining the type of pleasure and benefit are entirely out of one's own free choice, but follow the will of others, as they want, and not he. For example: I sit, I dress, I speak, and I eat. I do all these not because I want to sit that way, or talk that way, or dress that way, or eat that way, but because others want me to sit, dress, talk, and eat that way. It all follows the desire and fancy of society, not my own free will.

Furthermore, in most cases, I do all these against my will. For I would be a lot more comfortable behaving simply, without any burden. But I am chained with iron shackles, in all my movements, to the fancies and manners of others, which make up the society.

So you tell me, where is my freedom of will?

Baal HaSulam, "The Freedom"

A person alone will still want to eat, drink, sleep, and so on, even when there are no other people around him. However, if there are people around him, there is the matter of shame, where others compel him. Then he must eat and drink what people around him compel him to.

This is apparent primarily in clothing. At home, a person wears what is comfortable for him. But when he is among people, he must dress according to the way others see it. He has no choice, since shame compels him to follow their fancies.

Rabash, *Rabash—the Social Writings*,
"Mighty Rock of My Salvation"

Now you can understand the words of our sages about the verse, "Therefore choose life." It states, "I instruct you to choose the part of life, as one who says to his son: 'Choose for yourself a good part in my land.' He places him on the good part and tells him: 'Choose this for yourself.'" It is written about this, "O Lord, the portion of mine inheritance and of my cup, You maintain my lot. You placed my hand on the good fate, to say, 'This take for you.'"

The words are seemingly perplexing. The verse says, "therefore choose life." This means that one makes the choice by himself.

However, they say that He places him on the good part. Thus, is there no longer choice here? Moreover, they say that the Creator puts one's hand on the good fate. This is indeed perplexing, because if so, where then is one's choice?

Baal HaSulam, "Introduction to The Study of the Ten Sefirot," 4

Now you can see the true meaning of their words. It is indeed true that the Creator Himself puts one's hand on the good fate by giving him a life of pleasure and contentment within the corporeal life that is filled with torment and pain, and devoid of any content. One necessarily departs and escapes them when he sees a tranquil place, even if it seemingly appears amidst the cracks. He flees there from this life, which is harder than death. Indeed, there is no greater placement of one's hand by Him than this.

And one's choice refers only to the strengthening. This is because there is certainly a great effort and exertion here before one purifies one's body to be able to keep the Torah and *Mitzvot* correctly, not for his own pleasure, but to bring contentment to his Maker, which is called *Lishma* (for Her Name). Only in this manner is one endowed with a life of happiness and pleasantness that come with keeping the Torah.

However, before one comes to that purification there is certainly a choice to strengthen in the good way by all sorts of means and tactics. Also, one should do whatever his hand finds the strength to do until he completes the work of purification and will not fall under his burden midway.

Baal HaSulam, "Introduction to The Study
of the Ten Sefirot," Item 4

All of the indecent qualities in our nature, the Creator engrained in us and created us with all the lowliness.

Rabash, "Letter no. 29"

The Influence of the Environment on a Person

Thus, all [of man's] merit and spirit depends on the choice of the environment.

Baal HaSulam, "The Freedom"

Only in the matter of the choice of environment is man's reign over himself measured, and for this he should receive either reward or punishment.

Baal HaSulam, "The Freedom"

Obtaining the importance and exaltedness depends entirely on the environment.

Baal HaSulam, "A Speech for the Completion of The Zohar"

Only in that is one rebuked or praised—in his choice of environment. But once he has chosen the environment, he is at its hands as clay in the hands of the potter.

Baal HaSulam, "The Freedom"

There is freedom for the will to initially choose such an environment, such books, and such guides that impart to him good concepts. If one does not do that, but is willing to enter any environment that appears to him and read any book that falls into his hands, he is bound to fall into a bad environment or waste his time on worthless books, which are abundant and easier to come by. In consequence, he will be forced into foul concepts that make him sin and condemn. He will certainly be punished, not because of his evil thoughts or deeds, in which he has no choice, but because he did not choose to be in a good environment, for in that there is definitely a choice.

Baal HaSulam, "The Freedom"

He who strives to continually choose a better environment is worthy of praise and reward. But here, too, it is not because of his good thoughts and deeds, which come to him without his choice, but because of his effort to acquire a good environment, which brings him these good thoughts and deeds. It is as Rabbi Yehoshua Ben Perachya said, "Make for yourself a Rav, and buy for yourself a friend."

Baal HaSulam, "The Freedom"

Now you can understand the words of Rabbi Yosi Ben Kisma (*Avot* 6, 9), who replied to a person who offered him to live in his town, and he would give him thousands of gold coins for it: "Even if you give me all the gold and silver and jewels in the world, I will live only in a place of Torah." These words seem too sublime for our simple mind to grasp, for how could he relinquish thousands of gold coins for such a small thing as living in a place where there are no disciples of Torah, while he himself was a great sage who needed to learn from no one? Indeed, a mystery.

Baal HaSulam, "The Freedom"

Although everyone has "his own source" (initial essence) the forces are revealed openly only through the environment one is in. This is similar to the wheat sown in the ground, whose forces become apparent only through its environment, which is the soil, the rain, and the light of the sun.

Thus, Rabbi Yosi Ben Kisma correctly assumed that if he were to leave the good environment he had chosen and fall into a harmful environment, in a city where there is no Torah, not only would his former concepts be compromised, but all the other forces hidden in his source, which he had not yet revealed in action, would remain concealed. This is because they would not be subject to the right environment that would be able to activate them.

And as we have clarified above, only in the matter of the choice of environment is man's reign over himself measured, and for this he should receive either reward or punishment.

Baal HaSulam, "The Freedom"

The measure of the greatness does not depend on the individual, but on the environment. For example, even if one is filled with virtues but the environment does not appreciate one as such, one will always be low-spirited and will not be able to take pride in his virtues, although he has no doubt that they are true. And conversely, a person with no merit at all, whom the environment respects as though he is virtuous, that person will be filled with pride, since the measure of importance and greatness is given entirely to the environment.

Baal HaSulam, "A Speech for the Completion of The Zohar"

A person has qualities that his parents bequeathed to their children, and he has qualities that he acquired from the society, which is a new possession. And this comes to him only through bonding with the society and the envy that he feels toward the friends when he sees that they have better qualities than his own. It motivates him to acquire their good qualities, which he doesn't have and of which he is jealous.

Thus, through the society, he gains new qualities that he adopts by seeing that they are at a higher degree than his, and he is envious of them. This is the reason why now he can be greater than when he didn't have a society, since he acquires new powers through the society.

Rabash, *Rabash—the Social Writings*,
"Concerning Above Reason"

If one does not have any desire and craving for spirituality, if he is among people who have a desire for spirituality, if he likes these people, he, too, will take their strength to prevail, and their desires and aspirations, although by his own quality, he does not have these desires and cravings and the power to overcome. But according to the grace and the importance he ascribes to these people, he will receive new powers.

Baal HaSulam, *Shamati* [*I Heard*], Article no. 99,
"He Did Not Say Wicked or Righteous"

One cannot raise oneself above one's circle. Hence, one must suck from one's environment. And one has no other counsel, except through much work and Torah. Therefore, if one chooses for oneself a good environment, one saves time and efforts, since one is drawn according to one's environment.

Baal HaSulam, *Shamati* [*I Heard*], Article no. 225, "Raising Oneself"

Our sages said, "Make for yourself a rav and buy yourself a friend." This means that one can make a new environment for oneself. This environment will help him obtain the greatness of his rav through love of friends who appreciate the rav. Through the friends' discussing the greatness of the rav, each of them receives the sensation of his greatness. Thus, bestowal upon one's rav will become reception and sufficient motivation to an extent that will bring one to engage in Torah and *Mitzvot Lishma*.

They said about that, "The Torah is acquired by forty-eight virtues, by serving of sages and by meticulousness with friends." This is so because besides serving the rav, one needs the meticulousness of friends, as well, the friends' influence, so they will affect him the obtainment of his rav's greatness. This is so because obtaining the greatness depends entirely on the environment, and an individual cannot do a thing about it whatsoever.

Baal HaSulam, "A Speech for the Completion of The Zohar"

And while one sees how one's environment slights His work and does not properly appreciate His greatness, one cannot overcome the environment. Thus, one cannot obtain His greatness, and slights during one's work, as do they.

And since one does not have the basis for obtaining His greatness, he will obviously not be able to work to bestow contentment upon his Maker and not for himself. This is so because one would have no motivation to exert, and "if you did not labor and found, do not believe." And one's only choice is to either work for oneself or to not work at all, since for him, bestowing contentment upon one's Maker will not be tantamount to reception.

Now you can understand the verse, "In the multitude of people is the king's glory," since the measure of the greatness comes from the environment under two conditions:

1. The extent of the appreciation of the environment.
2. The size of the environment. Thus, "In the multitude of people is the king's glory."
   Baal HaSulam, "A Speech for the Completion of The Zohar"

The Freedom of the Collective and the Freedom of the Individual Are One

Therefore, the Tana (Rabbi Shimon Bar Yochai) described the Arvut as two people on a boat, when one of them began to drill a hole in the boat. His friend asked, "Why are you drilling?" He replied, "What business is it of yours? I am drilling under me, not under you." So he replied, "Fool! We will both drown together!"

Baal HaSulam, "The *Arvut* [mutual guarantee]," Item 18

Rabbi Elazar, son of Rabbi Shimon, says, 'Since the world is judged by its majority, and the individual is judged by the majority, if he performs one *Mitzva*, happy is he, for he has sentenced himself and the whole world to a scale of merit. If he commits one sin, woe unto him, for he has sentenced himself and the whole world to a scale of sin.'"

Baal HaSulam, "Introduction to The Study of the Ten Sefirot," Item 110

Do not be surprised that one person's actions bring elevation or decline to the whole world, for it is an unbending law that the general and the particular are as equal as two peas in a pod. And all that applies in the general, applies in the particular, as well. Moreover, the parts make what is found in the whole, for the general can appear only after the appearance of the parts in it, according to the quantity and quality of the parts. Evidently, the value of an act of a part elevates or declines the entire whole.

Baal HaSulam, "Introduction to The Book of Zohar," Item 68

And each and every individual in society is like a wheel that is linked to several other wheels, placed in a machine. And this single wheel has no freedom of movement in and of itself, but continues with the motion of the rest of the wheels in a certain direction, to qualify the machine to perform its general role.

And if there is some breakdown in the wheel, the breakdown is not evaluated relating to the wheel itself, but according to its service and role with respect to the whole machine.

Baal HaSulam, "Peace in the World"

Do not be surprised if I mix together the well-being of a particular collective with the well-being of the whole world, because indeed, we have already come to such a degree that the whole world is considered one collective and one society. Meaning, because each person in the world draws his life's marrow and his livelihood from all the people in the world, he is coerced to serve and care for the well-being of the whole world.

We have proven above that the total subordination of the individual to the collective is like a small wheel in a machine. He draws his life and his happiness from that collective, and therefore the well-being of the collective and his own well-being are one and the same, and vice-versa.

Baal HaSulam, "Peace in the World"

Therefore, in our generation, when each person is aided for his happiness by all the countries in the world, it is necessary that to that extent, the individual becomes enslaved to the whole world, like a wheel in a machine.

Therefore, the possibility of making good, happy, and peaceful conducts in one state is inconceivable when it is not so in all the countries in the world, and vice versa. In our time, the countries are all linked in the satisfaction of their needs of life, as individuals were in their families in earlier times. Therefore, we can no longer speak or deal with just conducts that promise the well-being of one country or one nation, but only the well-being of the whole world because the benefit or harm of each and every person in the world depends and is measured by the benefit of all the people in the whole world.

Baal HaSulam, "Peace in the World"

It thus turns out that the collective and the individual are one and the same. And the individual is not harmed because of his enslavement to the collective, since the freedom of the collective and the freedom of the individual are one and the same, too. And as they share the good, they also share the freedom.

Thus, good attributes and bad attributes, good deeds and bad deeds are evaluated only according to the benefit of the public.

Of course, the above words apply if all the individuals perform their role toward the public to the fullest and receive no more than they deserve, and take no more than their friends' share. But if a part of the collective does not behave accordingly, it turns out that not only do they harm the collective but they are also harmed.

We should not discuss further something that is known to all, and the aforesaid is only to show the drawback, the place that needs correction, and that is that each and every individual will understand that his own benefit and the benefit of the collective are one and same thing. In that, the world will come to its full correction.

Baal HaSulam, "Peace in the World"

And in our subject, the benefit of each and
every person within his collective is evaluated not according to his own goodness,
but according to his service to the public.
And vice-versa, we appreciate the attribute
of evil of each and every individual only according to the harm one inflicts upon the
public in general, and not by one's own individual value.

These things are crystal clear both from
the perspective of the truth in them, and
from the perspective of the good in them.
This is because what is found in the collective is only what is found in the individual.
And the benefit of the collective is the benefit of each and every individual: who harms
the collective takes his share in the harm, and
who benefits the collective takes his share in
the benefit, since individuals are part of the
whole, and the whole is not worth in any way
more than the sum of its individuals.

It thus turns out that the collective and the individual are one and the same. And the individual is not harmed because of his enslavement to the collective, since the freedom of the collective and the freedom of the individual are one and the same, too. And as they share the good, they also share the freedom.

Baal HaSulam, "Peace in the World"

The body with its organs are one. The whole of the body exchanges thoughts and sensations regarding each of its organs. For example, if the whole body thinks that a specific organ should serve it and please it, this organ will immediately know that thought and provide the contemplated pleasure. Also, if an organ thinks and feels that the place it is in is narrow, the rest of the body will immediately know that thought and sensation and move it to a comfortable place.

However, should an organ be cut off from the body, they will become two separate entities; the rest of the body will no longer know the needs of the separated organ, and the organ will not know the thoughts of the body, to benefit it and serve it. But if a physician came and reconnected the organ to the body as before, the organ would once again know the thoughts and needs of the rest of the body, and the rest of the body would once again know the needs of the organ.

Baal HaSulam, "A Speech for the Completion of The Zohar"

Now we can interpret what our sages wrote (*Hagiga* 15a), "Rewarded – a righteous. He takes his share and his friend's share in heaven. Convicted – a wicked. He takes his share and his friend's share in hell." It means that one takes the *Dinim* and the alien thoughts of one's friend, which we should interpret over the whole world, meaning that this is why the world was created filled with so many people, each with his own thoughts and opinions, and all are present in a single world.

It is so deliberately, so that each and every one will be incorporated in all of one's friend's thoughts. Thus, when one repents, the profit from it will be *Hitkalelut* (mingling/incorporation/integration).

It is so because when one wants to repent, one must sentence oneself and the entire world to a scale of merit, since he himself is incorporated in all the alien notions and thoughts of the entire world.

Baal HaSulam, *Shamati [I Heard]*, Article no. 33, "The Lots"

Is it possible that if someone sins or commits a sin that upsets his Maker, and you have no acquaintance with him, the Creator will collect his debt from you? It is written, "Fathers shall not be put to death for children... every man shall be put to death for his own sin" (Deuteronomy 24:16), so how can they say that you are responsible for the sins of even a complete stranger, of whom you know neither him nor his whereabouts?

And if that is not enough for you, see *Masechet Kidushin,* p 40b: "Rabbi Elazar, the son of Rabbi Shimon, says: 'Since the world is judged by its majority and the individual is judged by its majority, if he performed one *Mitzva,* happy is he, for he has sentenced the whole world to a scale of merit. And if he committed one sin, woe onto him, for he has sentenced himself and the whole world to a scale of sin, as it is said, 'one sinner destroys much good.'"

And Rabbi Elazar, son of Rabbi Shimon, has made me responsible for the whole world, since he thinks all the people in the world are responsible for one another, and each person brings merit or sin to the whole world with his deeds.

Baal HaSulam, *Matan Torah* [The Giving of the Torah], Item 17

The general and the particular are as equal two peas in a pod, both on the outer part of the world, meaning in the planets in general, and within it, for even within the smallest atom (molecule) of water, we find a complete system of sun and planets orbiting it, exactly as in the big world. Similarly, within man, the inner part of the world, you will find all the images of the Upper worlds: *Atzilut, Beria, Yetzira, Assiya*, as the Kabbalists have said that the *Rosh* is *Atzilut*, through the *Chazeh* it is *Beria*, from there to *Tabur* it is *Yetzira*, and below is *Assiya*.

Baal HaSulam, "The Meaning of Conception and Birth"

SPIRITUAL WORK IN THE GROUP

The Purpose of Society

We have gathered here to establish a society for all who wish to follow the path and method of Baal HaSulam, the way by which to climb the degrees of man and not remain as a beast.

The Rabash, *Rabash—the Social Writings*, "Purpose of Society (1)"

We gather here—to establish a society where each of us follows the spirit of bestowing upon the Creator. And to achieve bestowal upon the Creator, we must begin with bestowal upon man, which is called "love of others."

And love of others can only be through revoking of one's self. Thus, on the one hand, each person should feel lowly, and on the other hand, be proud that the Creator has given us the chance to be in a society where each of us has but a single goal: for Divinity to be among us.

The Rabash, *Rabash—the Social Writings*, "Purpose of Society (1)"

Each of us has but a single goal: for Divinity to be among us.

The Rabash, *Rabash—the Social Writings*, "Purpose of Society (1)"

We must remember that the society was established solely on the basis of achieving love of others, and that this would be the springboard for the love of God.

The Rabash, *Rabash—the Social Writings*,
"Concerning Love of Friends"

Obtaining the Greatness of the Creator through the Environment

The friends should primarily speak together about the greatness of the Creator.

The Rabash, *Rabash—the Social Writings*,
"What to Look For in the Assembly of Friends"

There is one point we should work on—*appreciation of spirituality*.

The Rabash, *Rabash—the Social Writings*,
"The Agenda of the Assembly"

Our sages said, "Make for yourself a rav and buy for yourself a friend." This means that one can make a new environment for oneself. This environment will help him obtain the greatness of his rav through love of friends who appreciate the rav. Through the friends' discussing the greatness of the rav, each of them receives the sensation of his greatness. Thus, bestowal upon one's rav will become reception and sufficient motivation to an extent that will bring one to engage in Torah and *Mitzvot Lishma*.

They said about that, "The Torah is acquired by forty-eight virtues, by serving sages and by meticulousness of friends." This is so because besides serving the rav, one needs the meticulousness of friends, as well, the friends' influence, so they will affect him the obtainment of his rav's greatness. This is so because obtaining the greatness depends entirely on the environment, and an individual cannot do a thing about it whatsoever.

Baal HaSulam, "A Speech for the Completion of The Zohar"

The whole basis upon which we can receive delight and pleasure, and which is permitted for us to enjoy—and is even mandatory—is to enjoy an act of bestowal. Thus, there is one point we should work on— *appreciation of spirituality*. This is expressed in paying attention to whom I turn, with whom I speak, whose commandments I am keeping, and whose laws I am learning, meaning in seeking advice concerning how to appreciate the Giver of the Torah.

And before one obtains some illumination from above by himself, he should seek out like-minded people, who are also seeking to enhance the importance of any contact with the Creator, in whatever way. And when many people support it, everyone can receive assistance from his friend.

The Rabash, *Rabash—the Social Writings*,
"The Agenda of the Assembly"

To the extent that the society regards the greatness of the Creator with their thoughts during the assembly, each according to his degree originates the importance of the Creator in him. At that time, each person's body feels that he regards anything that he wishes to do for holiness—meaning to bestow upon the Creator—as a great fortune, that he has been privileged with being among people who have been rewarded with serving the king. Thus, he can walk all day in the world of gladness and joy.

The Rabash, *Rabash—the Social Writings*,
"The Agenda of the Assembly"

And while one sees how one's environment slights His work and does not properly appreciate His greatness, one cannot overcome the environment. Thus, one cannot obtain His greatness, and slights during one's work, as do they.

And since one does not have the basis for obtaining His greatness, he will obviously not be able to work to bestow contentment upon his Maker and not for himself. This is so because one would have no motivation to exert, and "if you did not labor and found, do not believe." And one's only choice is to either work for oneself or to not work at all, since for him, bestowing contentment upon one's Maker will not be tantamount to reception.

Now you can understand the verse, "In the multitude of people is the king's glory," since the measure of the greatness comes from the environment under two conditions:

1. The extent of the appreciation of the environment.
2. The size of the environment. Thus, "In the multitude of people is the king's glory."
   Baal HaSulam, "A Speech for the Completion of The Zohar"

Unity of the Friends

You should know that there are many sparks of sanctity in each person in the group. When you collect all the sparks of sanctity into one place, as brothers, with love and friendship, you will certainly have a very high level of sanctity from the Light of Life, for the time being.

Baal HaSulam, *A Sage's Fruit*, Vol. 1, "Letter no. 13"

Each of them had a spark of love of others, but the spark could not ignite the light of love to shine in each, so they agreed that by uniting, the sparks would become a big flame.

The Rabash, *Rabash—the Social Writings*, "One Should Always Sell the Beams of His House"

I do remind you of the power of love of friends particularly at this time, for our existence depends on that, and this is the measure of our near-to-be success.

Therefore, turn away from all the imaginary engagements and set your hearts on contemplating thoughts and devising the right inventions to truly connect your hearts as one, and the words, "Love thy friend as yourself," will come true in you.

Baal HaSulam, *A Sage's Fruit*, Vol. 1, "Letter no. 47"

Do what you can and the salvation of the Lord is as a blink of the eye. And the most important matter before you this day is the unity of the friends. Exert in that as much as you can for it can compensate for all deficiencies.

Baal HaSulam, *A Sage's Fruit*, Vol. 1, "Letter no. 10"

I hereby instruct you to begin to love one another as yourselves, share your friend's sorrows and rejoice at your friend's delights as much as possible. I hope you will keep my words and carry out the matter in full.

Baal HaSulam, *A Sage's Fruit*, Vol. 1, "Letter no. 49"

This, too, I will ask of you: make great efforts in love of friends to find new ways to increase the love among the friends, and to nullify your bodily passions, for this is what casts hate, and among those bestowing contentment upon their Maker, no hate may be depicted. On the contrary, mercy and great love exists among them, and these words are simple.

Baal HaSulam, *A Sage's Fruit*, Vol. 1, "Letter no. 11"

Indeed, I feel all of you together, that you have replaced today with tomorrow, and instead of "now" you say, "later." There is no cure for that but to strain to understand that error and perversion—that only those who need salvation today are salvaged by the Creator. And those who can wait for tomorrow will obtain their wit after their years, God forbid. This came upon you due to your negligence in my request to exert in love of friends, as I have explained to you in every possible manner that this remedy is sufficient to complement for your every deficiency.

Baal HaSulam, *A Sage's Fruit*, Vol. 1, "Letter no. 13"

I have established orders for you, by which you can maintain the situation without regressing, and the most unique of which is adhesion of friends. I guarantee that this love is capable. I will remind you of everything good thing that you need; and if you are steadfast in that, come what may, you will surely go from strength to strength in spiritual ascensions.

Baal HaSulam, *A Sage's Fruit*, Vol. 1, "Letter no. 47"

"And a certain man found him, and behold, he was wandering in the field. And the man asked him, saying, 'What are you seeking?'" ... meaning, "How can I help you?" "And he said: 'I seek my brethren.'" By being together with my brothers, that is, by being in a group where there is love of friends, I will be able to mount the trail that leads to the house of God.

This trail is called "a path of bestowal," and this way is against our nature. To be able to achieve it, there is no other way but love of friends, by which everyone can help his friend.

The Rabash, *Rabash—the Social Writings*, "The Love of Friends"

There is none so wise as the experienced. Therefore, I will advise you to awaken within you fear of chilling the love between us, although the mind denies such an image. Still, exert yourself, if there is a tactic to increase the love, for one who does not add, it is regarded as decreasing, too. It is similar to one who gives a splendid gift to his friend; the love that appears in his heart at the time of action is unlike the love that remains in his heart after the fact. Rather, it gradually cools and wanes until one may completely lose the blessing of love. Thus, the recipient of the gift must find a way to make them new in his eyes each day.

Baal HaSulam, *A Sage's Fruit*, Vol. 1, "Letter no. 2"

How good and how pleasant it is for brothers to dwell together in unity. These are the friends, as they sit together inseparably. At first they look like people at war, wishing to kill each other, then they revert back to a state of brotherly love. The Creator, what does He say about them? "How good and how pleasant it is for brothers to dwell together in unity." The word "together" indicates the presence of Divinity with them. Moreover, the Creator listens to their discourse and He is pleased and content with them. And you, the friends who are here, just as you were previously in a state of love, so you should remain inseparable from now, until the Creator rejoices with you and calls peace upon you and by your merit shall there be peace in the world. "For the sake of my brothers and friends, I will say, 'May peace be within you.'"

The Book of Zohar with the *Sulam* [Ladder] commentary, *Aharei Mot*, Items 64-65

And while one begins to feel the love of his friend, joy and pleasure immediately begin to awaken in him, for the rule is that a novelty entertains. His friend's love for him is a new thing for him because he always knew that he was the only one who cared for his own well being. But the minute he discovers that his friend cares for him, it evokes within him immeasurable joy and he can no longer care for himself, since man can toil only where he feels pleasure. And since he is beginning to feel pleasure in caring for his friend, he naturally cannot think of himself.

Rabash, *Rabash—the Social Writings*, "Letter no. 40"

Each gift ... that he gives to his friend is like a bullet that makes a hollow in the stone. And although the first bullet only scratches the stone, when the second bullet hits the same place, it already makes a notch, and the third one makes a dent.

And through the bullets that he shoots repeatedly, the dent becomes a hollow in his friend's heart of stone, where all the presents gather. And each gift becomes a spark of love until all the sparks of love accumulate in the hollow of the stony heart and become a flame.

The difference between a spark and a flame is that where there is love, there is open disclosure, meaning a disclosure to all the peoples that the fire of love is burning in him. And the fire of love burns all the transgressions one meets along the way.

Rabash, *Rabash—the Social Writings*, "Letter no. 40"

And once I have acquired the clothing, sparks of love promptly begin to shine within me. The heart begins to long to unite with my friends, and it seems to me that my eyes see my friends, my ears hear their voices, my mouth speaks to them, the hands embrace, the feet dance in a circle, in love and joy together with them, and I transcend my corporeal boundaries. I forget the vast distance between my friends and me, and the outstretched land for many miles will not stand between us.

It is as though my friends are standing right within my heart and see all that is happening there, and I become ashamed of my petty acts against my friends. Then, I simply exit the corporeal vessels and it seems to me that there is no reality in the world except my friends and I. After that, even the "I" is cancelled and immersed, mingled in my friends until I stand and declare that there is no reality in the world—only the friends.

Rabash, *Rabash—the Social Writings*, "Letter no. 8"

One must know that love is bought by actions. By giving his friends gifts, each gift that he gives to his friend is like an arrow and a bullet, making a hole in his friend's heart. And although his friend's heart is like a rock, still, each bullet makes a hole. And the many holes join into a hollow, into which the love of the giver of presents enters.

And the warmth of the love draws to him his friend's sparks of love, and then the two loves weave into a garment of love that covers both of them. This means that one love surrounds and envelops the two, and they naturally become one person because the clothing in which they both cover is a single garment. Hence, both are annulled.

Rabash, *Rabash—the Social Writings*, "Man as a Whole"

The Power in Bonding

By the friends uniting into a single unit, they receive strength to appreciate the purpose of their work—to achieve *Lishma* [for Her name].

Rabash, *Rabash—the Social Writings*,
"The Need for Love of Friends"

If one does not have any desire and craving for spirituality, if he is among people who have a desire for spirituality, if he likes these people, he, too, will take their strength to prevail, and their desires and aspirations, although by his own quality, he does not have these desires and cravings and the power to overcome. But according to the grace and the importance he ascribes to these people, he will receive new powers.

Baal HaSulam, *Shamati* [*I Heard*], Article no. 99,
"He Did Not Say Wicked or Righteous"

There is a special power to adhesion of friends. Since the views and thoughts pass from one to the other through the adhesion between them, each is mingled with the power of the other, and by that, each person in the group has the power of the entire group. For this reason, although each person is an individual, he contains the power of the entire group.

Rabash, *Rabash—the Social Writings*,
"The Need for Love of Friends"

The advice for one to be able to increase his strength in the rule, "Love thy friend," is love of friends. If every one is nullified before his friend and mingles with him, they become one mass, where all the little parts that want the love of others unite in a collective force that consists of many parts. And when he has great strength, he can execute the love of others. And then he can achieve the love of God.

The Rabash, *Rabash—the Social Writings*, "According to What Is Explained Concerning 'Love Thy Friend as Thyself'"

According to what is written, "In the multitude of people is the king's glory," it follows that the greater the number of the collective, the more effective is the power of the collective. In other words, they produce a stronger atmosphere of greatness and importance of the Creator. At that time, each person's body feels that he regards anything that he wishes to do for holiness—meaning to bestow upon the Creator—as a great fortune, that he has been privileged with being among people who have been rewarded with serving the king. At that time, every little thing he does fills him with joy and pleasure that now he has something with which to serve the king.

The Rabash, *Rabash—the Social Writings*, "The Agenda of the Assembly"

A person has a desire within him, which comes from himself. In other words, even when he is alone and there are no people around him to affect him, or from whom to absorb some desire, he receives an awakening and craves to be a servant of the Creator. But his own desire is probably not big enough for him not to need to enhance it so he can work with it to obtain the spiritual goal. Therefore, there is a way—just like in corporeality—to enhance that desire through people on the outside who will compel him to follow their views and their spirit.

This is done by bonding with people whom he sees that also have a need for spirituality. And the desire that those people on the outside have begets a desire in him, and thus he receives a great desire for spirituality. In other words, in addition to the desire that he has from within, he receives a desire for spirituality that they beget in him, and then he acquires a great desire with which he can reach the goal.

The Rabash, *Rabash—the Social Writings*,
"Mighty Rock of My Salvation"

Principles of Spiritual Work in the Group

Love of friends that is built on the basis of love of others, by which they can achieve the love of the Creator, is the opposite of what is normally considered love of friends. In other words, love of others does not mean that the friends will love me. Rather, *it is I who must love the friends.*

The Rabash, *Rabash—the Social Writings,*
"What to Look For in the Assembly of Friends"

Each one should try to bring into the society a spirit of life and hopefulness, and infuse energy into the society. Thus, each of the friends will be able to tell himself, "Now I am starting a clean slate in the work." In other words, before he came to the society he was disappointed with the progress in the work of God, but now the society has filled him with life and hopefulness.

Thus, through society he obtained confidence and the strength to overcome because now he feels that he can achieve wholeness. And all his thoughts—that he was facing a high mountain that couldn't be conquered, and that these are truly formidable obstructions—now he feels that they are nothing. And he received it all from the power of the society because each and everyone tried to instill a spirit of encouragement and the presence of a new atmosphere in the society.

The Rabash, *Rabash—the Social Writings*,
"What to Look For in the Assembly of Friends"

Each student must extol the virtues of each friend and cherish him as though he were the greatest in the generation. Then the environment will affect him as a sufficiently great environment, since quality is more important than quantity."

The Rabash, *Rabash—the Social Writings*,
"What to Look For in the Assembly of Friends"

Each student must feel that he is the smallest among all the friends, and then he will be able to receive the appreciation of the greatness from everyone. This is so because the greater one cannot receive from the smaller one, much less be impressed by his words. Only the lower one is impressed by the appreciation of the greater one.

The Rabash, *Rabash—the Social Writings*,
"Concerning the Importance of Friends"

There should be careful watch in the society, disallowing frivolity among them, since frivolity ruins everything.

The Rabash, *Rabash—the Social Writings*,
"Purpose of Society (2)"

Rather, it is one person who can help another by seeing that one's friend is low. It is written, "One does not deliver oneself from imprisonment." Rather, it is one's friend who can uplift his spirit. This means that one's friend uplifts him from his state into a state of livelihood.

Then one begins to acquire confidence and wealth once more in life, and he begins as though his goal is now near him.

The Rabash, *Rabash—the Social Writings*,
"They helped Every One His Friend"

Those who have agreed among them to unite into a group understood that there isn't such a great distance between them in the sense that they understand the necessity to work in love of others. Therefore, each of them will be able to make concessions in favor of the others, and they can unite around that.

The Rabash, *Rabash—the Social Writings*,
"Make for yourself a Rav and Buy Yourself a Friend (2)"

To be integrated in one another, each person should annul himself before the others. This is done by each seeing the friends' merits and not their faults. But one who thinks that he is a little higher than the friends can no longer unite with them.

The Rabash, *Rabash—the Social Writings*,
"Purpose of society (2)"

It is a great effort when one should judge the friends to a scale of merit, and not everyone is ready for it.

Sometimes, it is even worse. At times, a person sees that his friend is disrespectful toward him. Even worse, he heard a slanderous rumor, meaning he heard from a friend that that friend, who is called so and so, said about him things that are not nice for friends to say about each other. Now he has to subdue himself and judge him to a scale of merit. This, indeed, is a great effort...

Therefore, when a person makes the effort and judges him to a scale of merit, it is a *Segula* [remedy/power/virtue], where by the toil that a person makes, which is called "an awakening from below," he is given strength from above to be able to love all the friends without exception.

This is called, "Buy yourself a friend," that a person should make an effort to obtain love of others.

The Rabash, *Rabash—the Social Writings*,
"What to Look For in the Assembly of Friends"

It turns out that each and every one must be attentive and think how he can help his friend raise his spirit, because regarding the mood, anyone can find a needy place in one's friend, which he can fill.

The Rabash, *Rabash—the Social Writings*,
"They Helped Every One His Friend"

He who thinks that he is deceiving his friend, is really deceiving the Creator, since besides man's body there is only the Creator. This is because it is the essence of creation that man is called "creature" only with respect to himself. The Creator wants man to feel that he is a separated reality from Him; but except for that, it is all "the whole earth is full of His glory."

Hence, when lying to one's friend, one is lying to the Creator; and when saddening one's friend, one is saddening the Creator.

Baal HaSulam, *Shamati [I Heard]*, Article no. 67,
"Depart from Evil"

Writers' Envy Increases Wisdom

A person has qualities that his parents bequeathed to their children, and he has qualities that he acquired from the society, which is a new possession. And this comes to him only through bonding with the society and the envy that he feels toward the friends when he sees that they have better qualities than his own. It motivates him to acquire their good qualities, which he doesn't have and of which he is jealous.

Thus, through the society, he gains new qualities that he adopts by seeing that they are at a higher degree than his, and he is envious of them. This is the reason why now he can be greater than when he didn't have a society, since he acquires new powers through the society.

Rabash, *Rabash—the Social Writings*,
"Concerning Above Reason"

Our sages said, "Counters' envy increases wisdom." In other words, when all the friends look at the society as being at a high level, both in thoughts and in actions, it is natural that each and every one must raise his degree to a higher level than he has by the qualities of his own body. ...Thus, now he has new qualities that society has procreated in him.

Rabash, *Rabash—the Social Writings*,
"Concerning Above Reason"

If he sees that the friends are at a higher degree than his own, he sees within reason how he is in utter lowliness compared to the friends, that all the friends keep the schedule of arriving at the seminary, and take greater interest in all that is happening among the friends, to help anyone in any way they can, and immediately implement every advice for the work from the teachers in actual fact, etc., it certainly affects him and gives him strength to overcome his laziness, both when he needs to wake up before dawn and when he is awakened. Also, during the lesson, his body is more interested in the lessons, since otherwise he will lag behind his friends.

Rabash, *Rabash—the Social Writings*,
"Concerning Above Reason"

When he sees that his friends are at a higher level than his own, this causes him to ascend in every way.

Rabash, *Rabash—the Social Writings*,
"Concerning Above Reason"

The Right Conduct at the Assembly of Friends

We should know that "Two is the least plural." This means that if two friends sit together and contemplate how to enhance the importance of the Creator, they already have the strength to receive enhancement of the greatness of the Creator in the form of awakening from below. And for this act, the awakening from above follows, and they begin to have some sensation of the greatness of the Creator.

The Rabash, *Rabash—the Social Writings*,
"The Agenda of the Assembly"

When they gather, what should they discuss? First, the goal must be clear to everyone—this gathering must yield the result of *love of friends*, that each of the friends will be awakened to love the other, which is called "love of others." However, this is only a result. To beget this lovely offspring, actions must be taken to produce the love.

The Rabash, *Rabash—the Social Writings*,
"What to Look For in the Assembly of Friends"

When they gather, each of them should think that he has now come for the purpose of annulling self-love. It means that he will not consider how to satisfy his will to receive now, but will think as much as possible only of the love of others. This is the only way to acquire the desire and the need to acquire a new quality, called "the will to bestow."

And from love of friends, one can reach love of the Creator, meaning wanting to give contentment to the Creator. It turns out that only in this does one obtain a need and understanding that bestowing is important and necessary, and this comes to him through love of friends.

The Rabash, *Rabash—the Social Writings*, "Love of Friends"

The beginning of the assembly, meaning the beginning of the discussions, which is the beginning of the assembly, should be about the praise of the society. Each and everyone must try to provide reasons and explanations to their merit and importance. They should speak of nothing but the praise of society.

Finally, its praise should be disclosed by all the friends. Then they should say, "Now we are through with stage one of the assembly of friends, and stage two begins." Then each will state his mind about the actions we can take so that each and everyone will be able to acquire the love of friends. In other words, *what each person can do to acquire love in his heart for each and everyone in the society.*

And once stage two is completed—which is suggestions regarding what can be done in favor of society—begins stage three. This concerns *carrying out of the friends' decisions about what should be done.*

The Rabash, *Rabash—the Social Writings*, "The Agenda of the Assembly"

PERCEPTION OF REALITY

Everything Is Preordained

We innovate nothing. Our work is only to illuminate what is hidden within man.
Rabbi Menahm Mendel of Kotzk

The same with one who has been granted the gift of knowing that he is the Creator's son; no change has been made in his actual reality but the awareness he had not had before.
Baal HaSulam, *The Writings of the Last Generation*

In the depth of the existence of the realistic life lies the answer, as it precedes the world. Prior to the sin, its repent was already prepared. Thus, there is nothing as certain in the world as repentance. At the very end, all will return to correction.
Rav Raiah Kook, *Orot HaTshuva [Lights of Repentance]*,
Chapter 6, Item 2

There is nothing more natural than coming into contact with one's Maker, for He owns nature. In fact, every creature has contact with his Maker, as it is written, "The whole earth is full of His glory," and not that one does not know and does not feel it.

Actually, one who attains contact with Him attains only the awareness. It is as though one has a treasure in his pocket, and he does not know. Along comes another who lets him know what is in his pocket, and now he really has become rich. Yet, there is nothing new here, no cause for excitation. In fact, nothing has been added.

Baal HaSulam, "The Solution"

The Creator truly resides within the heart of every person of Israel, and that is from His side. Hence, what does one lack? Only to know that. And the knowledge changes, and the knowing completes.

Baal HaSulam, *A Sage's Fruit*, Vol. 1, "Letter no. 32"

All is set ahead of time and each and every soul is already in all its Light, goodness, and eternity. It is only for the bread of shame that the soul came out restricted until it clothes in the murky body, and by its power does she return to her root prior to the restriction, with her rewarded from the whole of the terrible journey that she performed. And the entire reward is the real *Dvekut* [adhesion]. This means that she was rid of the bread of shame because her vessel of reception has become a vessel of bestowal and her form is equal to her Maker's.

Baal HaSulam, Letter no. 25

Similar to a teacher and a student, where the teacher's sole purpose is to provide the student with the power to be like him, and to teach other students like him. Similarly, the Creator has contentment when His creations create and renew, like Him. Indeed our whole power of renewal and development is not actual innovation. Rather, it is a kind of emulation, and our development is measured by the extent to which our emulation matches the work of nature.

Baal HaSulam, "The Meaning of Conception and Birth"

The thing is that by the very thought to create the souls, His thought completed everything, for He does not need an act, as do we. Instantaneously, all the souls and worlds that were destined to be created, emerged filled with all the delight and pleasure and the gentleness He had planned for them, in the final perfection that the souls were intended to receive at the end of correction, after the will to receive in the souls has been fully corrected and was turned into pure bestowal, in complete equivalence of form with the Emanator.

This is so because in His Eternalness, past, present, and future are as one. The future is as the present and there is no such thing as time in Him. Hence, there was never an issue of a corrupted will to receive in its separated state in *Ein Sof*.

On the contrary, that equivalence of form, destined to be revealed at the end of correction, appeared instantly in the Infinite. And our sages said about that: "Before the world was created there were He is One and His Name One," for the separated form in the will to receive had not been revealed in the reality of the souls that emerged in the Thought of Creation. Rather, they were cleaved unto Him in equivalence of form by way of, "He is One and His Name One."

Baal HaSulam, "Introduction to The Book of Zohar," 13

The Entire Reality Is Contained within Man

It is written in *The Zohar*, (*Vayikra*, *Parashat Tazria*, p 40), "Come and see, all that exists in the world, exists for man, and everything exists for him, as it is written, 'Then the

Lord God formed man,' with a full name, as we have established, that he is the whole of everything and contains everything, and all that is Above and below, etc., is included in man." Thus, it explains that all the worlds, Upper and lower, are included in man. And also, the whole of reality within those worlds is only for man.

Baal HaSulam, "Introduction to the Preface to the Wisdom of Kabbalah," Item 1

Take our sense of sight, for example: we see a wide world before us, wondrously filled. But in fact, we see all that only in our own interior. In other words, there is a sort of a photographic machine in our hindbrain, which portrays everything that appears to us and nothing outside of us.

Baal HaSulam, "Preface to the Book of Zohar," Item 34

For that, He has made for us there, in our brain, a kind of polished mirror that inverts everything seen there, so we will see it outside our brain, in front of our face. Yet, what we see outside us is not a real thing. Nonetheless, we should be so grateful to His Providence for having created that polished mirror in our brains, enabling us to see and perceive everything outside of us. This is because by that, He has given us the power to perceive everything with clear knowledge and attainment, and measure everything from within and from without.

Baal HaSulam, "Preface to the Book of Zohar," Item 34

Even though we see everything as actually being in front of us, every reasonable person knows for certain that all that we see is only within our own brains. So are the souls: Although they see all the images in the Giver, they still have no doubt that all these are only in their own interior, and not at all in the Giver.

Baal HaSulam, "Preface to the Book of Zohar," Item 34

We Have Neither Attainment Nor Perception of any Matter

We have no attainment or perception whatsoever in any substance, as all of our five senses are completely unfit for it. The sight, sound, smell, taste, and touch offer the scrutinizing mind mere abstract forms of "incidents" of the essence, formulating through collaboration with our senses.

Baal HaSulam, *The Study of the Ten Sefirot*, Part One, "Inner Reflection," Chapter 10

We have no perception whatsoever in the essence of the person in himself, without the matter. This is because our five senses and our imaginations offer us only manifestations of the actions of the essence, but not of the essence itself.

For example, the sense of sight offers us only shadows of the visible essence as they are formed opposite the light.

Similarly, the sense of hearing is but a force of striking of some essence on the air. And the air that is rejected by it strikes the drum in our ear, and we hear that there is some essence in our proximity.

The sense of smell is but air that emerges from the essence and strikes our nerves of scent, and we smell. Also, the sense of taste is a result of the contact of some essence with our nerves of taste.

Thus, all that these four senses offer us are manifestations of the operations that stem from some essence, and nothing of the essence itself.

Even the sense of touch, the strongest of the senses, separating hot from cold, and solid from soft, all these are but manifestations of operations within the essence; they are but incidents of the essence. This is so because the hot can be chilled; the cold can be heated; the solid can be turned to liquid through chemical operations, and the liquid into air, meaning only gas, where any discernment in our five senses has been expired. Yet, the essence still exists in it, since you can turn the air into liquid once more, and the liquid into solid.

Evidently, the five senses do not reveal to us any essence at all, but only incidents and manifestations of operations from the essence. It is known that what we cannot sense, we cannot imagine; and what we cannot imagine, will never appear in our thoughts, and we have no way to perceive it.

Baal HaSulam, "Preface to the Book of Zohar," Item 12

The thought has no perception whatsoever in the essence. Moreover, we do not even know our own essence. I feel and I know that I take up space in the world, that I am solid, warm, and that I think, and other such manifestations of the operations of my essence. But if you ask me about my own essence, from which all these manifestations stem, I do not know what to reply to you.

You therefore see that Providence has prevented us from attaining any essence. We attain only manifestations and images of operations that stem from the essences.

Baal HaSulam, "Preface to the Book of Zohar," Item 12

As there is no perception of the Creator whatsoever, so is it impossible to attain the essence of any of His creatures, even the tangible objects that we feel with our hands.

Thus, all we know about our friends and relatives in the world of action before us are nothing more than "acquaintance with their actions." These are prompted and born by the association of their encounter with our senses, which render us complete satisfaction although we have no perception whatsoever of the essence of the subject.

Furthermore, you have no perception or attainment whatsoever even of your own essence. Everything you know about your own essence is nothing more than a series of actions extending from your essence.

Baal HaSulam, "The Essence of the Wisdom of Kabbalah"

All Changes Are in the Desire, Not in the Light

We cannot attain any reality as it is in itself. Rather, we attain everything according to our sensations. And reality, as it is in itself, is of no interest to us at all. Hence, we do not attain the Torah as it is in itself, but only attain our sensations. Thus, all of our impressions follow only our sensations.

Baal HaSulam, *Shamati* [*I Heard*], Article no. 66, "The Giving of the Torah"

Therefore, we must not inquire how the sages of the Kabbalah, which fill the entire wisdom with their insights, differentiate between the various Lights. That is because these observations do not refer to the Lights themselves, but to the impression of the vessel, being the above-mentioned force, which is affected by its encounter with the Light.

Baal HaSulam, "The Wisdom of Kabbalah and Philosophy"

"There is no change in the Light." Rather, all the changes are in the *Kelim*, meaning in our senses. We measure everything according to our imagination. From this it follows that if many people examine one spiritual thing, each will attain according to his imagination and senses, thereby seeing a different form.

In addition, the form itself will change in a person according to his ups and downs, as we have said above that the Light is Simple Light and all the changes are only in the receivers.

Baal HaSulam, *Shamati [I Heard]*, Article no. 3,
"The Matter of Spiritual Attainment"

For themselves, all the worlds are regarded as simple unity and there is no change in

Godliness. This is the meaning of "I the Lord do not change." There are no *Sefirot* and *Behinot* (discernments) in Godliness. Even the most subtle appellations do not refer to the Light itself, as this is a discernment of *Atzmuto* where there is no attainment. Rather, all the *Sefirot* and the discernments speak only of what a person attains in them.

Baal HaSulam, *Shamati [I Heard]*, Article no. 3,
"The Matter of Spiritual Attainment"

The spiritual revelation, both the emerging from the concealment and any additions, extends primarily from the vessels and their power. It does not depend on the Upper Light whatsoever, for the rule is that there is no change in the actual Lights from the beginning of the line through the bottom of *Assiya*. As it is at the beginning of the line, it neither thickens nor changes when it is at the bottom of *Assiya*. It is also known that the Upper Light does not cease to bestow upon the lower ones even for a moment. Hence, the whole issue of concealment, revelation, changes, and every change, depends only on the power of the vessels.

Baal HaSulam, *The Bright Light*

The proliferation of the names is only with respect to the receivers. Hence, the first name that appeared, that is, the root for the creatures, is called *Ein Sof*. And this name remains unchanged. All the restrictions and the changes are made only with regard to the receivers, and He always shines in the first name, "His desire to do good to His creations," endlessly.

Baal HaSulam, *Shamati* [*I Heard*], Article no. 3,
"The Matter of Spiritual Attainment"

If you wish to say, "What are the *Sefirot* and the degrees in and of themselves?" We say that it is unattainable, since all of our attainment is only of His desire to do good to His creations. Hence, we can only attain that which concerns man, meaning man's impression from the Upper Light revealed to the creatures by the *Sefira*, but not the *Sefira* itself.

The multiplicity of *Sefirot* is only in the attainment of the lower ones, and depends on their qualification. Each one is uniquely qualified according to the quality of one's effort. Other than that, everything is equal, for there are no changes in spirituality. This is why we say regarding the *Sefirot* themselves that they are completely imperceptible by thought.

Rabash, "Letter no. 19"

We can only speak from where our senses are impressed by the expanding Light, which is "His desire to do good to His creations," which comes into the hands of the receivers in actual fact.

Similarly, when we examine a table our sense of touch feels it as something hard. We also discern its length and width, all according to our senses. However, that does not necessitate that the table will appear so to one

who has other senses. For example, in the
eyes of an angel, when it examines the table,
it will see it according to *its* senses. Hence, we
cannot determine any form with regard to an
angel, since we do not know its senses.

Baal HaSulam, *Shamati [I Heard]*, Article no. 3,
"The Matter of Spiritual Attainment"

All these images and changes begin and end
only with the impression of the souls.

Baal HaSulam, "Preface to the Book of Zohar," Item 33

There is no change at all in the world *Atzilut*
itself, whether the lower ones receive its great
abundance lushly, or receive nothing at all.
The above-mentioned greatness lies solely on
the lower ones.

Baal HaSulam, "Preface to the Book of Zohar," Item 32

When the Light of *Malchut* descends and
expands over the people. At that time, it
appears to them, to each and every one, according to their own appearance, vision, and

imagination, meaning only in the receivers and not at all in the *Sefira Malchut* herself.

Baal HaSulam, "Preface to the Book of Zohar," Item 35

A Thought Is an Upshot of the Desire

The desire is the root of the mind and not the mind the root of desire.

Baal HaSulam, "Peace in the World"

The thought serves the desire, and the desire is the "self" of the person.

Baal HaSulam, *Shamati* [*I Heard*], Article no. 153,
"The Thought Is an Upshot of the Desire"

The mind is enslaved and serves the desire.

Baal HaSulam, "Introduction to The Book of Zohar," Item 21

A thought is an upshot of the desire. A person thinks of what he wants, and does not think of what he does not want. For example, a person never thinks of his dying day. On the contrary, he will always contemplate his eternity, since this is what he wants. Thus, one always thinks of what is desirable for him.

However, there is a special role to the thought: it intensifies the desire. The desire remains in its place; it does not have the strength to expand and perform its action. Yet, because one thinks and contemplates on a matter, and the desire asks of the thought to provide some counsel and advice to carry out the desire, the desire thus grows, expands and performs its actual work. It turns out that the thought serves the desire, and the desire is the "self" of the person. Now, there is a great self or a small self. A great self dominates the small selves.

He who is a small self and has no dominion whatsoever, the advice to magnify the self is through the persisting with the thought of the desire, since the thought grows to the extent that one thinks of it.

And so, "in His law doth he meditate day and night," for by persisting in it, it grows into a great self until it becomes the actual ruler.

Baal HaSulam, *Shamati [I Heard]*, Article no. 153, "The Thought Is an Upshot of the Desire"

The very essence of the soul is a will to receive, as well. And the difference we can tell between one object and another is discerned only by its will.

Baal HaSulam, "Introduction to The Book of Zohar," Item 21

Time and Motion

Spirituality depends on neither time nor place, and there is no death there.

The Writings of Baal HaSulam, "From within my Flesh shall I see God"

In truth, *The Zohar* speaks nothing of corporeal incidents, but of the upper worlds, where there is no sequence of times as it is in corporeality. Spiritual time is elucidated by change of forms and degrees that are above time and place.

The Book of Zohar with the *Sulam* [Ladder] commentary, *VaYetze*, Item 139

Indeed, you should know that spiritual movement is not like tangible movement from place to place. Rather, it refers to a renewal of form, for we denominate every renewal of form by the name "movement."

Baal HaSulam, *The Study of the Ten Sefirot*, Part 1, "Inner Reflection," Chapter 9

The spiritual definition of time: Understand that for us, the spiritual definition of time is only a sensation of movements. Our imagination pictures and devises a certain number of movements, which it discriminates one by one and translates them like a certain amount of "time." Thus, if one had been in a state of complete rest with one's environment, he would not even be aware of the concept of time.

Baal HaSulam, *The Study of the Ten Sefirot*, Part One, Inner Reflection, Chapter 9

The present and the future are divided within the truth of being. That which has been is that which shall be, and that which has been done is that which shall be done. That which has already been done and that which shall be done in the future is gradually being done in the present, constantly and frequently.

Rav Raiah Kook, *Orot HaKodesh* (*Lights of Sanctity*), 2 p 373

Any content of time, even the general terms of past and future, is only one of the ways of human reasoning. With respect to Above, it is completely irrelevant. Hence, anything potential is completely unreal without the actual, from the perspective of the absolute Upper reality. Indeed, anything in potential is executed in time, and the continuation of time is irrelevant regarding the Upper. Thus, we can say, "That which will be is already present."

Whoever draws his desire and the depths of his life close to the exaltedness of sublime, Divine adhesion, which stands at the top of the world, above the succession of times, to the same extent of his ascension are the

differences between potential and realization—
and inevitably between future and present—
become faint, until they do not part at all.

Rav Raiah Kook, *Igrot [Letters]*, Vol. 2, p 38

Incarnation of Souls

In our world, there are no new souls the way
bodies are renewed, but only a certain amount
of souls that incarnate on the wheel of transformation of the form, because each time they
clothe a new body and a new generation.

Baal HaSulam, "The Peace"

Although we see the bodies changing from
generation to generation, this is only the case
with the bodies. But the souls, which are the
essence of the body's self, do not vanish, to be
replaced, but move from body to body, from
generation to generation. The same souls
that were at the time of the flood came also
during the time of Babylon, and in the exile

in Egypt, and in the exodus from Egypt, etc., until this generation and until the end of correction.

Baal HaSulam, "The Peace"

With regard to the souls, all generations since the beginning of Creation to the end of correction are as one generation that has extended its life over several thousand years, until it developed and became corrected as it should be. And the fact that in the meantime each has changed its body several thousand times is completely irrelevant, because the essence of the body's self, called "the soul," did not suffer at all by these changes.

Baal HaSulam, "The Peace"

The eternal soul of life that the Creator had blown in his nostrils, only for the needs of *Adam ha Rishon*, has departed because of the sin of the Tree of Knowledge. It acquired a new form, called "Sweat of Life," meaning the general has been divided into a great many particulars, tiny drops, divided between *Adam ha Rishon* and all his progeny through the end of time.

It follows, that there are no changes in the acts of the Creator, but there is rather an additional form here. This common Light of life, which was packed in the nose of *Adam ha Rishon* has expanded into a long chain, revolving on the wheel of transformation of form in many bodies, body after body, until the necessary end of correction.

Baal HaSulam, "Introduction to the Book,
Panim Meirot uMasbirot," Item 22

THE GREATNESS OF
BAAL HASULAM

And God said unto me: "Get thee out of thy country, to the pleasant land, the land of the Holy Fathers, where I will make you a great sage and all the sages of the land shall be blessed in you, for I have chosen you for a righteous sage in all this generation, to heal the human suffering with lasting salvation. Take this sword in your hand, and guard it with thy heart and soul, for it is a sign between Me and you, that all those good things will happen through you, for until now, I had no such faithful man as you, to give him this sword.

Baal HaSulam, "The Prophecy of Baal HaSulam"

For a long time now, my conscience has burdened me with a demand to come out and create a fundamental composition regarding the essence of Judaism, religion, and the wisdom of Kabbalah, and spread it among the nation, so people will come to know and properly understand these exalted matters in their true meaning.

Baal HaSulam, "Time to Act"

Know for sure that since time of the Ari to this day, there has not been anyone to understand the heart of the method of Ari. It was easier to acquire a mind twice as holy and great as the Ari's than to comprehend his method, which has been held by many, from the first one who heard and documented it, to the latest compilers, while they did not attain the matters fully, at their Highest source, and each one confused the matters and mixed them up.

And yet, by a High Will, I have been rewarded with an impregnation of the soul of The Ari, not for my own good deeds, but by a High Will. It is beyond my grasp, as well, why

I have been chosen for this wonderful soul, which no man has been rewarded with since his demise until today. I can not expand on this issue, as it is not my way to speak of the wondrous.

Baal HaSulam, *A Sage's Fruit*, Vol. 1, "Letter no. 39"

And after all these days, I listened attentively to all the promises and destinies I have been chosen for by the Creator. Yet, I found in them neither satisfaction nor the words by which to speak to the dwellers of this world and to lead them to God's will, as He had told me to. I could not stride among the people, who are vain and slandering the Creator and His creation, while I was satiated and praising, merrily walking, as though mocking those wretched ones.

Matters have touched me to the bottom of my heart, and I resolved that come what may, even if I descend from my sublime degree, I must make a heartfelt plea to the Creator, to grant me attainment and knowledge of the prophecy and wisdom, and the words by which to help the forlorn people of the world, to raise them to the same degree of wisdom and pleasantness as mine. And although I knew that I must not sadden my spirit, I could not stand by, and I poured my heart out in prayer.

Baal HaSulam, "The Prophecy of Baal HaSulam"

The Creator has found me favorable in His Eyes to reveal to me all the lowliness of the generation, and all sorts of easy and reliable corrections, to bring each soul to its root at the utmost speed.

Baal HaSulam, *A Sage's Fruit*, Vol. 1, "Letter no. 9"

I am glad that I have been born in such a generation when it is permitted to disclose the wisdom of truth. And should you ask, "How do I know that it is permitted?" I will reply that I have been given permission to disclose. Until now, the ways by which it is possible to publicly engage and to fully explain each word have not been revealed to any sage. And I, too, have sworn by my teacher not to disclose, as did all the students before me. However, this oath and this prohibition apply only to those manners that are given orally from generation to generation, back to the prophets and before. Had these ways been revealed to the public, they would cause much harm, for reasons known only to us.

Yet, the way in which I engage in my books is a permitted way. Moreover, I have been instructed by my teacher to expand it as much as I can. We call it "the manner of clothing the matters." You will see in the writings of Rashbi that he calls this way, "giving permission," and this is what the Creator has given me to the fullest extent. We deem it as dependent not on the greatness of the sage, but on the state of the generation, as our sages said, "Little Samuel was worthy, etc., but his generation was unworthy." This is why I said that my being rewarded with the manner of disclosing the wisdom is because of my generation.

Baal HaSulam, "The Teaching of the Kabbalah and Its Essence"

And who better than I knows that I am not at all worthy of being even a messenger and a scribe for disclosing such secrets, and much less to thoroughly understand them. And why has the Creator done so to me? It is only because the generation is worthy of it, as it is the last generation, which stands at the threshold of complete redemption. And for this reason, it is worthy of beginning to hear the voice of Messiah's *Shofar*, which is the revealing of the secrets, as has been explained.

Baal HaSulam, "Messiah's *Shofar* [horn]"

I am the first interpreter by root and branch, and cause and consequence. Hence, if one were to understand some matter through my commentary, one can be certain that everywhere this matter appears in *The Zohar* and in the

Tikkunim, he can be assisted by it, as with the commentaries on the literal, where you can be assisted by one place for all the other places.

Baal HaSulam, "The Teaching of the Kabbalah and Its Essence"

Because faith has generally diminished, specifically faith in the holy men, the wise men of all generations. And the books of Kabbalah and *The Zohar* are filled with corporeal parables. Therefore, people are afraid lest they will lose more than they will gain, since they could easily fail with materializing. And this is what prompted me to compose a sufficient interpretation to the writings of the Ari, and now to the Holy *Zohar*. And I have completely removed that concern, for I have evidently explained and proven the spiritual meaning of everything, that it is abstract and devoid of any corporeal image, above space and above time, as the readers will see, to allow the whole of Israel to study *The Book of Zohar* and be warmed by its sacred Light.

Baal HaSulam, "Introduction to The Book of Zohar," Item 58

All the interpretations of *The Book of Zohar* before ours did not clarify as much as ten percent of the difficult places in *The Zohar*. And in the little they did clarify, their words are almost as abstruse as the words of *The Zohar* itself.

But in our generation we have been rewarded with the *Sulam* (Ladder) commentary, which is a complete interpretation of all the words of *The Zohar*. Moreover, not only does it not leave an unclear matter in the whole of *The Zohar* without interpreting it, but the clarifications are based on a straightforward analysis, which any intermediate student can understand. And since *The Zohar* appeared in our generation, it is a clear proof that we are already in the days of the Messiah, at the outset of that generation upon which it was said, "for the earth shall be full of the knowledge of the Lord."

Baal HaSulam, "A Speech for the Completion of The Zohar"

And here I come to praise my father and teacher, whose holy words shine in our generation, the generation of darkness and concealment. And concerning the concealment and revelation, I heard from him, the holy one, on the eve of *Sukkot*, 1942, in Jerusalem, when he entered the *Sukkah* to see if it was properly built.

... And if one corrects the discernment of waste of barn and winery, the discernment of *Malchut, MAN de Nukva*, considered the seventh millennium, one is rewarded with the tenth millennium, considered *GAR*. Such a soul comes down to the world once every ten generations. Thus far the content of his holy words.

From these holy words we can understand the greatness of the soul of my father and teacher, and his degree while saying them. He had told me several times that he had never said words of Torah without first attaining the words of Torah from inside the degree.

Rabash, introduction to the book, *A Sage's Fruit*, Vol. 2

Baal HaSulam promised us that by walking in his path and keeping his instructions, we will be rewarded with His eternity, cleaving to Him and entering the hall of the King.

Baal HaSulam, *A Sage's Fruit*, Vol. 1, "Letter no. 29"

Even if we were rewarded with hearing the words of the living God directly from Baal HaSulam, we would still have a place for choice. Thus, even though he disclosed many revelations to us, it was only to guide us, so we may walk unassisted.

Baal HaSulam, *A Sage's Fruit*, Vol. 1, "Letter no. 28"

Baal HaSulam made it so that if a simple person walked in his path, he could achieve the same *Dvekut* [adhesion] with the Creator as that of an outstanding wise disciple. Before him, one had to be an outstanding wise disciple to be rewarded with *Dvekut* with the Creator. And before the Baal Shem Tov, one had to be among the greatest in the world. Otherwise, they would not be able to attain Godliness.

Rabash, *Steps of the Ladder*, "The Deeds of the Nation's Greatest"

This is what I have troubled to do in this interpretation, to explain the ten *Sefirot* as the Godly sage the Ari had instructed us, in their spiritual purity, devoid of any tangible terms. Thus, any beginner may approach the wisdom without failing in any materialization and mistake. With the understanding of these ten *Sefirot*, one will also come to examine and know how to comprehend the other issues in this wisdom.

Baal HaSulam, *The Study of the Ten Sefirot*, Part 1, "Inner Reflection"

With these words I unbind myself from a considerable complaint, that I have dared more than all my predecessors in disclosing the ordinarily covered rudiments of the wisdom in my book, which was thus far unexplored. This refers to the essence of the ten *Sefirot* and all that concerns them, *Yashar* and *Hozer*, *Pnimi* and *Makif*, the meaning of the *Hakaa* and the meaning of the *Hizdakchut*.

The authors that preceded me deliberately scattered the words here and there, and in subtle intimations, so one's hand would fail to gather them. I, through His Light, which appeared upon me, and with the help of my teachers, have gathered them and disclosed the matters clearly enough and in their spiritual form, above place and above time.

Baal HaSulam, "Introduction to the Book, Panim Meirot uMasbirot," Item 5

The depth of wisdom in the holy *Book of Zohar* is enclosed and caged behind a thousand locks, and our human tongue too poor to provide us with sufficient, reliable expressions to interpret one thing in this book to its end. Also, the interpretation I have made is but a ladder to help the examiner rise to the height of the matters and examine the words of the book itself. Hence, I have found it necessary to prepare the reader and give him a route and an inlet in reliable definitions concerning how one should contemplate and study the book.

Baal HaSulam, "Preface to the Book of Zohar," Item 1

There is a strict condition during the engagement in this wisdom – to not materialize the matters with imaginary and corporeal issues. This is because thus they breach, "Thou shalt not make unto thee a graven image, nor any manner of likeness."

In that event, one is rather harmed instead of receiving benefit. Therefore, our sages cautioned to study the wisdom only after forty years, or from a Rav, and other such cautions. All of that is for the above reason.

To rescue the readers from any materialization, I compose the book *Talmud Eser Sefirot* (*The Study of the Ten Sefirot*) by the Ari.

Baal HaSulam, "Introduction to The Study of the Ten Sefirot," Item 156

Here I would briefly say that in this general preface, I wish to give the student a true and general knowledge of the majority of this expansive wisdom, and true orientation in the style of study in the book, *The Tree of Life*.

Most students fail to understand the matters, since the spiritual concepts are above time and above place, but they are expressed in corporeal terms, pictured and set in times and places.

Additionally, in the writings of the Ari, no order for beginners is arranged in this wisdom. The books were composed by the holy words that he would say before his students day-by-day, and the students themselves were proficient in the wisdom of truth. Hence, there is no text—long or short—in all the books that were written, which does not require true proficiency in the wisdom in general. For this reason, the students grow weary and cannot connect matters altogether.

Thus, I have come out with this preface, to connect the matters and the foundations of the wisdom in a concise manner, so it will be readily available to the student with every text he may wish to study in the writings of the Ari.

Baal HaSulam, "General Preface to the Book, Panim Meirot uMasbirot," Item 1

KABBALISTS
CITED IN THIS BOOK

RABBI ABRAHAM EBEN EZRA, RAABA (1089-1164)

Rabbi Abraham Eben Ezra, *Raaba*: one of the great sages of Spain; spent his entire life wandering. He composed dozens of essays on different subjects: Poetry, grammar, commentary, astrology, etc.. Among his books are *Yesod Mora* [*The Foundation of Fear*] *HaMispar* [*The Number*], *HaIbur* [*Conception*], *Safa Brurah* [*Clear Language*], *HaTe'amim* [*The Taamim*], *Reishit Hochmah* [*The Beginning of Wisdom*].

RABBI ABRAHAM BEN MORDECHAI AZULAI (1570-1644)

Rabbi Abraham Ben Mordechai Azulai: A Kabbalist Rabbi from Fez, Morocco, whose family was banished from Spain in 1492. He immigrated to Israel in 1615 and died in Hebron. Rabbi Haim David Yosef Azulai, *Ha-Hida*, who was one of his descendants, wrote words of praise about him. Rabbi Abraham Azulai composed several Kabbalah books, including *Ohr HaChama* [*Light of the Sun*], *Hesed L'Avraham* [*Mercy unto Abraham*], *Zoharei Hama* [*Radiance of the Sun*]—an abridged version of Rabbi Abraham Glanati's Commentary to the Zohar, *Baalei Brit Avraham* [*Abraham's Allies*].

RAV ABRAHAM ISAAC HACOHEN KOOK, HARAIAH KOOK (1865-1935)

Rabbi Abraham Isaac HaCohen Kook was among the greatest sages of Israel in the last one hundred years. For many, the image of the *Rav Kook* symbolized the transition from the exile to The Land of Israel. He was Chief Rabbi of "Boysk Yeshiva," and in 1904 moved from "Volozhin Yeshiva" to Jerusalem, where he served as the first Chief Ashkenazi Rabbi in The Land of Israel.

The Rav Kook had a great impact on the Jewish education in Israel, attempting to unite the different factions and reviving the approach to the research and study of Judaism. The Rav Kook supported the study of the wisdom of the hidden and was one of Rav Yehuda Ashlag's (Baal HaSulam) friends.

His teachings are extensively detailed in many books, such as: *Orot HaKodesh* [*Lights of Sancitty*] vols. 1, 2, 3, *Letters* vols. 1, 2, 3, *Essays of the Raiah*, *Orot* [*Lights*], *Orot HaTorah* [*Lights of the Torah*], *Orot Hateshuva* [*Lights of Repentance*], and numerous others.

THE GAON [GREAT SCHOLAR] RABBI ELIJAH, GRA, THE VILNA GAON (1720-1797)

The Vilna Gaon, GRA, lived his entire life in Vilna. He was one of the greatest sages and was extremely knowledgeable in general, particularly in sciences. The Vilna Gaon composed more than seventy books interpreting The Bible, which excelled in their simplicity and clarity. GRA became known as the greatest opposer to the *Hassidut* movement. He wished to move to The Land of Israel and even began his journey there. However, due to hardships on the way, he returned to Vilna. A group of his disciples carried out his instruction and founded the congregation of the *Prushim* [seclusive].

RABBI BARUCH BEN ABRAHAM OF KOSOV
(...-1792)

Rabbi Baruch Ben Avraham of Kosov, a Kabbalist from the sages of Poland, from the first generation of the *Hassidut*, a student of Rabbi Menahem Mendel of Vitebsk and the *Maggid* [Sayer] of Mezeritch. He composed two Kabbalah books: *Pillar of the Work* and *Foundation of the Faith*, commentaries on the Torah.

Rav Baruch Shalom Ashlag, Rabash (1907-1991)

Rav Baruch Shalom Ashlag (Rabash) was the eldest son and follower of Rav Yehuda Leib HaLevi Ashlag (Baal HaSulam). From the young age of nine, he began to study with his father, joining him on his trips to the Rabbi of Porsov and the Rabbi of Belz.

In 1921, Rabash immigrated to Israel along with his father, and at the age of twenty, he was ordained to the Rabbinate by the High Court of Justice of the ultra-orthodox congregation and the Chief Rabbi of Jerusalem, Rabbi Chaim Zonenfeld, Rabbi Yaakov Moshe Harlap, and Rav Raiah Kook. By so doing, he received, in compliance with his father's demand, ordainment from both the ultra-orthodox and the Zionist movement.

Rabash studied Kabbalah with his father for many years and began teaching at his father's request. Following the demise of Baal

HaSulam, Rabash became the leader of the congregation, at his students' request. Rabash dedicated his life to disseminating the unique path of Baal HaSulam and to expanding the interpretation and explanation of his method.

Prior to his death, Rabash gave his student and follower, Rav Michael Laitman, a notebook within which he had documented his father's words as he had heard them. Those notes have been published in the book *Shamati* [*I Heard*]. The group Bnei Baruch [Sons of Baruch], which was founded by Rav Michael Laitman for the purpose of disseminating his path, is named after Rav Baruch Shalom Ashlag.

RABBI CHAIM BEN YITZHAK OF VOLOZHIN (1749-1821)

Rabbi Chaim Ben Yitzhak of Volozhin was one of the great Kabbalists, the students of the Vilna Gaon (GRA). He founded the great Yeshiva of Volozhin under GRA's instruction.

His books: *Nefesh HaChaim* [*Soul of Life*] discusses morals, *Ruach Chaim* [*Spirit of Life*] interprets *Pirkei Avot* [*Ethics of the Fathers*].

RABBI CHAIM DAVID YOSEF AZULAI, "HACHIDA" (1724-1806)

Rabbi Chaim David Yosef Azulai (HaChida) was born in Jerusalem and died in Livorno. He was a *Halachah* [religious law] adjudicator and a Kabbalist, a historian and a bibliographer. HaChida journeyed most of his life and was one of the first Hebrew bibliographers.

HaChida served as a Rabbi in Egypt for five years and visited Turkey, Greece, Italy, France, England, and Germany, among others. Wherever he traveled, he researched and searched for ancient scripts, from which he copied important details, writing them in a diary called *Good Circle*. HaChida composed numerous books, including *Holding the Blessing*, *Joseph's Blessings*, *Sought Life*, and *The Courage of Joseph*.

RAV CHAIM VITAL (1543-1620)

Rav Chaim Vital, one of the great Kabbalists in Safed, the personal disciple and the sole follower of Rabbi Yitzhak Luria, The *Ari*.

Chaim Vital was born in Safed and died in Damascus. He was the student of Rabbi Moshe Alshich and Rabbi Moshe Cordovero (Ramak). In 1570, upon the Ari's arrival in Safed, Rabbi Chaim Vital recognized his greatness and the uniqueness of his method and became his personal student. For a year and a half, he meticulously documented the words and customs of the Ari.

Prior to his passing in 1572, the Ari instructed all of his students to forget what he had taught them, except Chaim Vital. He specifically indicated that Chaim Vital was the only one allowed to continue to study his special method. In 1594, he moved to Damascus and lived there for the rest of his life. His writings were hidden and buried by his side as he had instructed. However, they were later removed from the grave and were published by members of his family.

His famous book *The Tree of Life*, describes the method of the Ari. Among other published writings are *Eight Gates to the Ari*, within which are "Gates of Reincarnation," "Gate of Intentions," "Gate of Introductions." Additional published writings include *The Book of the Treasures of Life*, *Four Hundred Silver Shekels*, and *Book of Visions*.

RABBI YEHUDA ASHLAG, BAAL HASULAM (1884-1954)

Rav Yehuda Ashlag, known as Baal HaSulam for his authoritative *Sulam* [Ladder] commentary on *The Book of Zohar*, as it served as a ladder to rise to complete goodness. Baal HaSulam was born in Poland and was educated by the Rabbi of Kloshin and the Rabbi of Porsov. He served as an adjudicator in Warsaw and immigrated to Israel in 1921, where he served as the rabbi of Givat Shaul and engaged in the study, interpretation, and dissemination of the wisdom of Kabbalah his entire life.

Baal HaSulam developed a new method of studying Kabbalah, allowing all those interested in reaching spiritual attainment to use it. In addition to composing the *Sulam* commentary on *The Zohar*, he explained and interpreted the writings of the Ari in his book, *The Study of the Ten Sefirot*.

In 1933, he published the book *Matan Torah* [*The Giving of the Torah*], in which he compiled articles on the topic of Kabbalah which he published in a newspaper. Baal HaSulam composed a series of introductions preparing the student for proper study of texts of Kabbalah and explaining the way of study. Among his compositions are "Introduction to The Book of Zohar," "Introduction to The Study of the Ten Sefirot," *Panim*

Meirot ve Masbirot [a commentary on *The Tree of Life*], Or HaBahir [*Bright Light*], Beit Shaar HaKavanot [*Gatehouse of Intentions*], Pri Hacham [*A Sage's Fruit*].

RABBI YOSEF ELIEZER ROSENFELD
(...-1915)

Rabbi Yosef Eliezer Rosenfeld, a sage from Poland, was appointed as the Rabbi of Preishtetl in 1890. He composed the books *Chavat Yair* [*Havot Yair*] and *Ateret Tzvi* [*A Crown of Glory*].

RABBI YAACOV TZEMACH

Rav Yaacov Tzemach, a Kabbalist, a student of Rav Shmuel Vital, son of Rav Chaim Vital. Rav Yaacov Tzemach was born in Lisbon and immigrated to Jerusalem via Damascus. He composed several books, including a well-known commentary on the writings of the Ari, *Kol BeRamah* [*A Voice in Ramah*], an abridged version of the intention of the Ari, called *Nagid UMetzaveh* [*A Leader and Commander*], *Olat HaTamid* [*The Continual Burnt Offering*], on the intention of Rav Chaim Vital, *Tzemach Tzadik* [*The Righteous Tzemach*].

RABBI YITZCHAK ISAAC YEHUDA YECHIEL SAFRIN OF KOMARNO (1806-1874)

Rabbi Yitzchak Yehiel of Komarno became well-known for his extensive knowledge of the hidden and revealed Torah. He was educated in the surroundings of the Seer of Lublin, Rabbi Naftali of Rufshitz, and Rabbi Abraham Mordechai of Pintschov. He composed many books including *Maase Ereg* [*Woven Work*] and *Atzei Eden* [*Trees of Eden*] on the Mishnah, *The Face of the Elder* on *Masechet Shekalim*, *The Treasure of Life and the Hall of Blessing*, *Notzer Hesed* [*Treasuring Mercy*], *Zohar Chai* [*Living Brightness*], and *Netiv Mitzvotecha* [*Path of Your Commandments*].

Rabbi Yitzhak Ben Tzvi Ashkenazi
(...-1806)

Rabbi Yitzhak Ben Tzvi Ashkenazi was the chief justice in Hodorov, Poland, and later an adjudicator in Levov. His famous book *Purity of Sanctity*, which discusses *Masechet Zevachim*, proved his depth in the laws and in Kabbalah. He composed another book called *The Candlelight*.

Rabbi Yitzhak Luria Ashkenazi, Ari (1534-1572)

The Ari disclosed and developed a new method of studying Kabbalah, called "The Lurianic method." The Ari was born in Jerusalem. His father died when he was young, and his mother traveled with him to her brother Rabbi Mordechai Francis, who lived in Egypt. The Ari studied Torah and Kabbalah with Rabbi David Even Zimra, Radbaz, and with Rabbi Bezalel Ashkenazi. He was secluded himself for seven years, studying *The Book of Zohar*.

In 1570, the Ari went to the Kabbalist city of Safed. The great Kabbalists, old and young, who realized the greatness and uniqueness of his method, wished to study with him, but he turned some of them down. For a year and a half, he taught his students the principles of his method, yet before his passing, he instructed them not to engage in it. Only his student Rav Chaim Vital was allowed to teach his method, since he was the only one who understood it properly.

The Ari taught his students orally and did not leave any notes after him. However, Chaim Vital, who documented his words meticulously, composed the books *The Tree of Life* and *Eight Gates to the Ari*, based on the notes. The writings of Chaim Vital were buried next to him but members of his family later dug them out and published his books.

The Ari composed several poems, found in the *Siddur* [prayer book], including *Azamer*

BeShvachin [I Will Sing in Praise], *Bnei Heichala* [Sons of the Palace], *Asader LiSeudata* [I Will Set Up for the Meal].

RABBI ISRAEL BAAL SHEM TOV, [THE BAASHT (BAAL SHEM TOV)] (1698-1760)

The Baal Shem Tov, Rabbi Israel Ben Eliezer Baal Shem Tov, founder of the Hassidic movement, was born in Poland. His parents died when he was young. In his youth he used to seclude himself in the mountains and study Kabbalah. He wandered around Poland gathering Jews in whom he found a special drive to know the purpose of their lives. After teaching them how to attain spirituality, he founded and led the Hassidic movement with their help.

The Baasht stood out in his unique and charismatic personality. He introduced a new kind of Jewish leadership, the *Tzadik* [a righteous man]. The Baasht also fashioned the model of a group uniting around a charismatic leader who gives personal guidance to each of his disciples.

The *Hassidut* emphasized the intention of the heart and the enthusiasm more than studiousness and erudition. It emphasized the person's attainment of the Creator by himself or with the help of a *Tzadik*. His words were quoted in many books, including *Keter Shem Tov* [*The Crown of Shem Tov*], *Meirot Einayim* [*Opening the Eyes*], and *Tzava'at Ribash* [*The Will of Ribash*].

RABBI MENAHEM MENDEL OF KOTZK
(1787-1859)

Rabbi Menahem Mendel of Kotzk was born in Goraj near Lublin, Poland. He grew up in a home of opposers to Hassidism, yet already from a young age was drawn to *Hassidut* and studied with Rabbi Simcha Bonim of Pshischa, Rabbi Yaacov Yitzhak, the Jew from Pshischa, and the Seer of Lublin.

He was poignant and original in his approach and became well-known for his precise and razor-sharp sayings. He demanded a true and serious approach toward spirituality, focusing the majority of one's effort on the goal of life. Among his well-known disciples were Rabbi Yitzhak Meir of Gur, author of *Hidushei HaRIM* [*Innovations of the RIM*], Rabbi Hanoch Hanich of Alexander, Rabbi Ze'ev Wolf of Starikov, and Rabbi Yehiel Meir of Gustanin.

His many students continued his unique path in Hassidic congregations that they founded throughout Eastern Europe. In 1840, the Rabbi of Kotzk isolated himself and refused to come in contact even with his disciples. Many books were written about him and his sharp tongue and discernments, such as, "There is none so whole as a broken heart," in *A bush burns in Kotzk*.

RABBI MENAHEM NACHUM TWERSKY
OF CHERNOBYL (1730-1798)

Rabbi Menahem Nachum Twersky of Chernobyl was educated in the Lita [Lithuania] Seminary and was influenced by the teachings of the Ari. He was a student of The Baal Shem Tov, and after his demise he studied with the Sayer of Mazritch. He was an Admor [a great teacher] of the first generation of *Hassidut*. Rabbi Twersky founded the *Hassidut* dynasty in Chernobyl. His books are *The Light of the Eyes* on the Torah, *Let the Heart Rejoice*, literal interpretations of the Gemarah according to Kabbalah.

RABBI MOSHE BEN MAIMON,
RAMBAM [MAIMONIDES] (1138-1204)

Maimonides was among the greatest adjudicators and Jewish philosophers in the Middle Ages, a leader and a physician. He was born in Kordova, Spain, and moved to North

Africa. After writing the composition *Kiddush Hashem* [*Sanctification of the Creator*], he was forced to leave with the *Anusim* ["forced ones": terminology applied to a Jew who has been forced to abandon Judaism against one's will] and arrived in Israel.

As a result of the difficult living conditions in the country, he moved to Egypt, serving as physician and counselor to one of the most important rulers. His status allowed him to serve as governor of the Egyptian Jews.

Among his compositions are *Hilchot Deot, Hilchot Avoda Zara* [*Laws of Idolatry*], *Guide to the Perplexed, Perush Mishnahyot* [*Commentaries on the Mishnah*], *Mishneh Torah, Sefer HaMitzvot* [*The Book of Commandments*], *Teshuvot BeHalacha* [*Answers on Laws*], "Letters of Maimonides, the Glory of the Generation (Q&A)."

RABBI MOSHE CHAIM EPHRAIM OF SADILKOV (1748-1800)

Rabbi Mosh Haim Efraim, author of the book *The Banner of the Camp of Ephraim*, was the Baal Shem Tov's grandson and became known as the Rabbi of Sadilkov. He was born in the town of Mazhibozh and studied with his grandfather, the Baasht. After the passing of the Baasht, he studied with the Sayer of Mazritch and Rabbi Yaacov Yosef from Polana. Afterward, he settled in Sadilkov. His book, *The Banner of the Camp of Ephraim*, is one of the seminal books of *Hassidut*, accurately describing the words of the Baal Shem Tov.

RABBI MOSHE CHAIM LUZATO, THE RAMCHAL (1707-1747)

Rabbi Moshe Chaim Luzato, The Ramchal, was a great and well-known Kabbalist from Italy. He was born in Padua and was particularly outstanding from a very young age in his rare memory and ability for deep study.

At only fourteen years of age, he had already the entirety of the writings of the Ari's. At the age seventeen, he wrote his first book and was fiercely opposed by Rabbi Hagiz. In 1740, he published his renowned book *Mesilat Yesharim* [*Path of the Just*]. In 1743, he immigrated to The Land of Israel and died of a plague in Acre along with his entire family. He composed some forty books among which are *Klalei Pitchei Hochmah VeDaat* [*Rules of the Doors of Wisdom and Knowledge*], *Shaarey Ramchal* [*Gates of Ramchal*], and *Adir BaMarom* [*The Mighty One on High*].

Rabbi Moshe Cordovero, Ramak (1522-1570)

Rabbi Moshe Cordovero, Ramak, was among the sages in the land of Israel. He lived most of his life in Safed and was a student of Rabbi Yosef Karo, and the

Kabbalist Rabbi Shlomo Elkabetz, compos-
er of the psalm *Go My Beloved.*

At age twenty six, he wrote his first book
Pardes Rimonim [*Orchard of Pomegranates*],
which discusses the wisdom of Kabbalah.
Prior to the arrival of the Ari in Safed, Ramak was considered the greatest Kabbalist of
Safed. Among his students were Eliahu di Vi-
dash, author of *Resheet Hochma* [*Beginning of
Wisdom*], and Rabbi Abraham Glenati, com-
poser of *Kol Bochim* [*Voice of the Wailing*].

Ramak published several other books,
the most well-known being *Ohr Yakar* [*Precious Light*], an extensive and profound commentary on *The Zohar.* Some of that extensive
commentary was published with the title
Shiur Komah [*A Measure of Height*], an introduction to the interpretation of the *Idrot* [*As-
semblies*] of *The Zohar.* Additional books are
Ohr Ne'erav [*Evening Light*], *Sefer HaGirushin*
[*Book of the Expelled*], *Sefer Ilima Rabati* [*Book*

of the Great Ilima], *A Prayer unto Moses*, and *Know the God of Your Father*.

RABBI NACHMAN OF BRESLEV
(1772-1810)

Rabbi Nachman of Breslev was Baal Shem Tov's grandson. In 1798 he immigrated to Israel, yet, because of Napoleon's wars, he returned to the Ukraine, settled in the town of Uman and taught *Hassidut* through tales and stories. Some of his compositions are *Talks of Rabbi Nachman*, and *Likutey Moharan* [*Collections of Teacher Rabbi Nachman*].

RABBI PINCHAS ELIYAHU BEN MEIR
(...-1802)

Rabbi Pinchas Eliyahu Ben Meir composed *Sefer HaBrit* [*Book of the Covenant*] anonymously. He also composed *Mitzvot Tovim* [*Commandment of the Good*], discussing the purpose of the *Mitzvot* [commandments], *Beit Yotzer* [*Birthplace*], which interprets *Sefer*

Yetzira [Book of Craetion], Matmonei Mistorim [Hidden Treasures], concerning letter combinations and an interpretation of Rabbi Emanuel Chai Riki's book Mishnat Hassidim [Teaching of the Hassidim].

RABBI TZVI HIRSH EICHENSTEIN OF ZIDITSHOV (1763-1831)

Rabbi Tzvi Hirsh Eichenstein of Ziditshov, son of Rabbi Yitzhak Isaac of Safrin, Hungary, was a student of The Seer of Lublin's and was considered one of his heirs. Among others, he studied with the Sayer of Kuznitch, Rabbi Elimelech of Lizhanski, Rabbi Moshe Leib of Sassov, Rabbi Yehoshua Hashil of Afta, and Rabbi Baruch of Mazbozh. He was well-known in the revealed Torah and the concealed Torah and composed the books Ateret Tzvi [A Crown of Glory], a commentary on The Zohar, Sur MeRa VeAseh Tov [Depart from Evil and Do Good], Beit Yisrael [The House of Israel], and Pri Kodesh Hilulim [Holy Fruit for Praising].

RABBI SHALOM BEN MOSHE BUZZAGLO
(...-1780)

Rabbi Shalom Ben Mosh Buzzaglo, a famous Kabbalist from Marrakesh, Morocco, a student of Rabbi Abraham Ben Mordechai Azulai, composed several Kabbalah books. Among them are *Kisse HaMelech* [*The King's Throne*], a commentary on the *Tikkunim* [corrections] of *The Zohar*, *Hadrat Melech* [*King's Glory*], a commentary on *The Zohar* divided into two Chapters: *Hod Melech* [*The King's Majesty*] on *Safra de Tzniuta*, and *Mikdash Melech* [*The King's Temple*] and *Kisse Melech* [*The King's Throne*] on the *Tikkunim*.

RABBI SIMCHA BONIM OF PSHISCHA
(1767-1827)

Rabbi Simch Bonim of Pshischa, the son of Rabbi Yitzhak HaMaggid, was born in Vadislav. In his youth, he studied with Rabbi Mordechai Bennett. He was introduced to *Hassidut* and became one of the leaders of the second generation of the *Hassidut*. He was a student of the Seer of Lublin, Rabbi Yaacov Yitzhak and the Holy Jew, Rabbi Yaacov Yitzhak of Pashicsa.

He continued the path of the Holy Jew, delving and expanding the path of *Hassidut*. His well-known students were Rabbi Menachem Mendel of Kotzk, Rabbi Yitzcak of Vorka, *Hidushey HaRim*–the Rabbi of Gur, Rabbi Yehezkel of Kozmir, Rabbi Chanoch Hanich of Alexander, Rabbi Abraham of Tscheknov, and others.

His teachings were published in his students' books, *Hedvat Simcha* [*Joy of Gladness*], *Ramatim Tzofim* [*The Low of Joy*], *Ramathaim-Zophim*, and *Kol Simcha* [*The Voice of Joy*].

RABBI SHIMON BEN LAVI
(1488-1588)

Kabbalist Rabbi Shimon Ben Lavi was born in Spain and was exiled with his family in 1492.

He roamed Portugal and in 1497, moved to Fez in Morocco. In 1549 he moved to Tripoli, where he became the Community Rabbi. Rabbi Shimon Ben Lavi composed poems on Rashbi and two books, *Ketem Paz* [*Spot of Gold*], and *Yad Ne'eman* [*Faithful Hand*].

RABBI SHIMON BAR YOCHAI, RASHBI

Rabbi Shimon Bar Yochai, Rashbi, one of the most prominent student of Rabbi Akiva, is mentioned in the Mishnah numerous times as "Rabbi Shimon," and is well known in the revealed Torah and the concealed Torah.

Rashbi grew up in Yavne and was ordained by Rabbi Akiva and Rabbi Yehuda Ben Baba to teach the wisdom of Kabbalah to the future generations. Following Rabbi Akiva's incarceration, the government was informed that he was speaking against them so he hid in a cave in Peki'in for thirteen years, along with his son, Rabbi Elazar.

Following his exit from the cave, Rabbi Shimon gathered nine students, went with them into a small cave in Meron, and with their help, he wrote *The Book of Zohar*, the seminal book of Kabbalah. However, he instructed his student Rabbi Abba to do the actual writing, since he knew that he was the only one who could conceal what needed to be concealed and reveal what was revealed. When he composed *The Book of Zohar*, he knew it was intended for future generations so he hid it.

The Book of Zohar was written in a special language, the language of *Midrash*, Aramaic. In *The Zohar* itself, it is mentioned that Aramaic is the posterior of Hebrew. *The Zohar* is regarded as the foundation of the wisdom of Kabbalah. It describes a clear and formulated method to attain spirituality and is taught by people the world over. Rav Yehuda Ashlag's authoritative commentary, *Perush HaSulam* [*The Sulam Commentary*], enables its study in our time as well.

Rabbi Shimon Bar Tzemach Duran, Rashbatz (1361-1444)

Rabbi Shimon Bar Zemach Duran, Rashbatz, was a physician, a poet and a Kabbalist. He studied with Rabbi Nissim Ben Reuven and with Rabbi Yitzhak Bar Sheshet (the Ribash). He lived in Spain, but moved to Algeria during the persecution in Spain in 1391. Rashbatz composed many books and was outstanding in its questions and answers which were published in the three volumes of *Tashbetz* [Crossword]. Additional books include *Magen Avot* [The Fathers' Shield], *Ohr HaChaim* [Light of Life], *Leviat Chen* [A Graceful Wreath], *Yavin Shmua* [Understanding Rumors], and *Zohar HaRakia* [Brightness of the Firmament].

Rabbi Schneier Zalman of Laddi, The Old Admor (1745-1813)

Rabbi Schneier Zalman of Laddi, the old Admor, founded *Hassidut* Habad, despite the Vilna Gaon's (GRA) objection. Rabbi

Schneier studied Kabbalah and *Hassidut* with the Sayer of Mazritch and founded his method in *Hassidut* called *HaBaD*, (*Hochma, Bina, Daat*) after the passing of the Sayer of Mazritch.

During the war between Russia and France in 1812, he convinced his students to support Russia and later had to escape the vengeance of the French. He composed the books *Shulhan Aruch HaRav* [*The Rav's Set Table*] an updated book of laws for the *Habad Hassidim*, which is still in use today, *Siddur Tefila* [*Prayer Book*], *Likutei Torah* [*Collections of Torah*], and *The Tanya* [*Tanya Rabbati*], describing the foundations of his method.

RESEARCHERS AND PHILOSOPHERS WRITE ABOUT KABBALAH

JOHANNES REUCHLIN
(1455-1522)

Reuchlin, a German humanist, political counselor to the Chancellor, a classics scholar and an expert in the ancient languages and traditions (Latin, Greek, and Hebrew) was affiliated with the heads of the Platonic Academia (della Mirandola and others).

"My teacher Pythagoras, who is the father of philosophy, did nevertheless not receive those teachings from the Greeks, but rather he received them from the Jews. Therefore he must be called 'a Kabbalist,' [...] and he himself was the first to convert the name

'Kabbalah,' unknown to the Greeks, in the Greek name philosophy."

"Pythagoras' philosophy emanated from the infinite sea of the Kabbalah"

"The Kabbalah does not let us spend our lives on the ground, but rather raises our intellect to the highest goal of understanding."
Reuchlin, *De Arte Cabbalistica*

GIOVANNI PICO DELLA MIRANDOLA
(1463-1494)

An Italian scholar and Neoplatonist philosopher whose *De Hominis Dignitate Oratio* (*Oration on the Dignity of Man*), composed in 1486, was a characteristic Renaissance work. It reflected his syncretistic method of taking the best elements from other philosophies and combining them in his own work. Additionally, della Mirandola researched Kabbalah, the Bible, and the Koran after reading them in their original languages.

"This true interpretation of the law (*vera illius legis interpretatio*), which was revealed to Moses in godly tradition, is called Kabbalah (*dicta Cabala est*), which to Hebrews is the same as for us receiving (*receptio*)."

"In whole [there are] two sciences - also with a name they honored them: the one is called *ars combinandi* and it is a measure of the progress in sciences [...]. The other one treats the forces of the higher things, which are over the moon, which is the highest part of *magia naturalis*. The Hebrews also call both of them Cabala [...]"

Pico della Mirandola, *Conclusions*

Paulus Ricius
(~1470-1541)

Ricius, a physician and a professor of philosophy at Pavia University, Austria, served as personal physician and consultant to Maximilian I, Archduke of Austria, German King and Holy Roman emperor, and to Ferdinand I—King of Bohemia and Hungary.

"The ability to interpret the divine and human secrets by a type of the Mosaic law with allegorical sense is called Kabbalah."

"A literal meaning (of a Scripture) submits to the conditions of time and space. Allegorical and kabbalistic - remains for centuries, unbounded by time and space."

Paulus Ricius, *Introductoria Theoramata Cabalae*

PHILIPPUS AUREOLUS PARACELSUS
(1493-1541)

A German-Swiss physician and alchemist, Paracelsus established the role of chemistry in medicine. He is considered one of the founders of modern science.

"Learn artem cabbalisticam, it explains everything!"

Paracelsus, *Das Buch Paragranum*

CHRISTIAN KONRAD SPRENGEL
(1750-1816)

A German botanist and teacher whose studies of reproduction in plants led him to a general theory of fertilization which is still accepted today.

"Adam, the first man, was very familiar with the Kabbalah. He knew the signatures of all things, and hence gave all animals the most suitable names ... which themselves indicate their nature."

Kurt Sprengel, *Versuch einer Pragmatischen Geschichte der Arzneikunde*

RAYMUNDUS LULLUS
(1235-1315)

Lullus, a Spanish writer and philosopher born to a wealthy family in Palma, Mallorca, was well educated, and became the tutor of King James II of Aragon. He wrote in Arabic, Latin and Catalan. He wrote treatises on alchemy and botany, Ars Magna, and Llibre de meravelles.

"Creation, or language, are of equal weight in the science of Kabbalah. Because Creation or language are root of the regulation of everything, it is clear that its wisdom governs the rest of the sciences."

"Sciences such as theology, philosophy and mathematics receive their principles and roots from her. And therefore these sciences (scientiae) are subordinate to that wisdom (sapientia); and their [the sciences] principles and rules are subordinate to her [Kabbalah] principles and rules; and therefore their [the sciences] mode of argumentation is insufficient without her [the Kabbala]."

Raymundus Lullus, *Raymundi Lulli Opera Latina*

GIORDANO BRUNO
(1548-1600)

An Italian philosopher, astronomer, mathematician, and occultist who was ahead of his time. His theories anticipated modern science. The most notable of these were his theories of the infinite universe and the multiplicity of worlds, in which he rejected the traditional geocentric (Earth-centered) astronomy and intuitively went beyond the Copernican heliocentric (Sun-centered) theory, which still maintained a finite universe with a sphere of fixed stars. Bruno is, perhaps, chiefly remembered for the tragic death he suffered at the stake. A victim of his own beliefs, he maintained his unorthodox ideas when both the Roman Catholic and the Reformed churches were reaffirming rigid Aristotelian and Scholastic principles.

"The Kabbalah first gives an inexpressible name to the highest principle; from it she lets four principles emanate in an emanation of second degree, from which everyone branches out again to twelve [...] as there are innumerable kinds and subspecies. And in such a way they designate with a special name, depending upon their language, a God, an angel, a reason, a power, which governs over each individual species. In this way it is finally revealed that the whole divinity can be affiliated to one original Source, as well as the whole light, which shines originally and independently, and the images, which break in numerous different mirrors as in just as many individual objects can be led back to a formal and ideal principle, the source of those images."

Giordano Bruno, *Le Opere Italiane*

GOTTFRIED WILHELM LEIBNITZ
(1646-1716)

Leibnitz was a German philosopher, mathematician, and Imperial Court Counselor to the Habsburgs, important both as a metaphysician and as a logician and distinguished also for his independent invention of the differential and integral calculus. In 1661 he entered the University of Leipzig as a law student; there he encountered the ideas of men who had revolutionized science and philosophy, such as Galileo, Francis Bacon, Thomas Hobbes, and René Descartes. In 1666 he wrote *De Arte Combinatoria* (*On the Art of Combination*), in which he formulated a model that is the theoretical ancestor of modern computers.

"Since people did not possess the right key to the secret, the thirst for knowledge eventually led to vanities and superstition of all kinds, from which ultimately developed a kind of Vulgar Cabbala that lies far away from the true one, as well as diverse fantastic theories under the false name of magic; the books are teeming with those."

Leibnitz, *Hauptschriften zur Grundlegung der Philosophie*

FRIEDRICH VON SCHLEGEL
(1772-1829)

German writer, critic and philosopher, contemporary of Goethe, Schiller and Novalis. A pioneer in comparative Indo-European linguistics and comparative philology, Schlegel deeply influenced the early German Romantic Movement. He is generally held to be the person who first established the term *romantisch* in the literary context.

"The true esthetics is Kabbalah (quote from December, 1802)."
Schlegel, *Kritische F. Schlegel-Ausgabe, publisher: Ernst Behler 35 Bde., Paderborn*

JOHANN WOLFGANG VON GOETHE
(1749-1832)

Johann Wolfgang Goethe is widely recognized as the greatest writer of the German tradition. The Romantic period in Germany (late eighteenth and early nineteenth centuries) is known as the Age of Goethe, and Goethe embodies the concerns of the generation defined by the legacies of Jean-Jacques Rousseau, Immanuel Kant, and the French Revolution. His stature derives not only from his literary achievements as a lyric poet, novelist, and dramatist, but also from his often significant contributions as a scientist (geologist, botanist, anatomist, physicist, historian of science) and as a critic and theorist of literature and art. For the last thirty years of his life he was Germany's greatest cultural icon, serving as an object of pilgrimage from all over Europe and the United States.

"The kabbalistic treatment of the Bible is a hermeneutics, which lives up in a convincing way to the independence, the marvelous originality, the versatility, the totality, I would even say immeasurability of its contents."

Goethe, *Materialien zur Geschichte der Farbenlehre*

Further Reading

Attaining the Worlds Beyond

From the introduction to *Attaining the Worlds Beyond*: "...Not feeling well on the Jewish New Year's Eve of September 1991, my teacher called me to his bedside and handed me his notebook, saying, 'Take it and learn from it.' The following morning, he perished in my arms, leaving me and many of his other disciples without guidance in this world.

"He used to say, 'I want to teach you to turn to the Creator, rather than to me, because He is the only strength, the only Source of all that exists, the only one who can really help you, and He awaits your prayers for help. When you seek help in your search for freedom from the bondage of this world, help in elevating yourself above this world, help in finding the self, and help in determining your purpose in life, you must turn to the Creator, who sends you all those aspirations in order to compel you to turn to Him.'"

Attaining the Worlds Beyond holds within it the content of that notebook, as well as other inspiring texts. This book reaches out to all those seekers who want to find a logical, reliable way to understand the world's phenomena. This fascinating introduction to the wisdom of Kabbalah will enlighten the mind, invigorate the heart, and move readers to the depths of their souls.

SHAMATI

Rav Michael Laitman's words on the book: Among all the texts and notes that were used by my teacher, Rav Baruch Shalom Halevi Ashlag (the Rabash), there was one special notebook he always carried. This notebook contained the transcripts of his conversations with his father, Rav Yehuda Leib Halevi Ashlag (Baal HaSulam), author of the *Sulam* (Ladder) commentary on *The Book of Zohar*, *The Study of the Ten Sefirot* (a commentary on the texts of the Kabbalist, Ari), and of many other works on Kabbalah.

Not feeling well on the Jewish New Year's Eve of September 1991, the Rabash summoned me to his bedside and handed me a notebook, whose cover contained only one word, *Shamati* (I Heard). As he handed the notebook, he said, "Take it and learn from it." The following morning, my teacher perished in my arms, leaving me and many of his other disciples without guidance in this world.

Committed to Rabash's legacy to disseminate the wisdom of Kabbalah, I published the notebook just as it was written, thus retaining the text's transforming powers. Among all the books of Kabbalah, *Shamati* is a unique and compelling creation.

KABBALAH FOR THE STUDENT

Kabbalah for the Student offers authentic texts by Rav Yehuda Ashlag, author of the *Sulam* (Ladder) commentary on *The Book of Zohar*, his son and successor, Rav Baruch Ashlag, as well as other great Kabbalists. It also offers illustrations that accurately depict the evolution of the Upper Worlds as Kabbalists experience them. The book also contains several explanatory essays that help us understand the texts within.

In *Kabbalah for the Student*, Rav Michael Laitman, PhD, Rav Baruch Ashlag's personal assistant and prime student, compiled all the texts a Kabbalah student would need in order to attain the spiritual worlds. In his daily lessons, Rav Laitman bases his teaching on these inspiring texts, thus helping novices and veterans alike to better understand the spiritual path we undertake on our fascinating journey to the Higher Realms.

RABASH—THE SOCIAL WRITINGS

Rav Baruch Shalom HaLevi Ashlag (Rabash) played a remarkable role in the history of Kabbalah. He provided us with the necessary final link connecting the wisdom of Kabbalah to our human experience. His father and teacher was the great Kabbalist, Rav Yehuda Leib HaLevi Ashlag, known as Baal HaSulam for his *Sulam* (Ladder) commentary on *The Book of Zohar*. Yet, if not for the essays of Rabash, his father's efforts to disclose the wisdom of Kabbalah to all would have been in vain. Without those essays, few would be able to achieve the spiritual attainment that Baal HaSulam so desperately wanted us to obtain.

The writings in this book aren't just for reading. They are more like an experiential user's guide. It is very important to work with them in order to see what they truly contain. The reader should try to put them into practice by living out the emotions Rabash so masterfully describes. He always advised his students to summarize the articles, to work with the texts, and those who attempt it discover that it always yields new insights. Thus, readers are advised to work with the texts, summarize them, translate them, and implement them in the group. Those who do so will discover the power in the writings of Rabash.

THE SCIENCE OF KABBALAH

Kabbalist and scientist Rav Michael Laitman, PhD, designed this book to introduce readers to the special language and terminology of the authentic wisdom of Kabbalah. Here, Rav Laitman reveals authentic Kabbalah in a manner both rational and mature. Readers are gradually led to understand the logical design of the Universe and the life that exists in it.

The Science of Kabbalah, a revolutionary work unmatched in its clarity, depth, and appeal to the intellect, will enable readers to approach the more technical works of Baal HaSulam (Rabbi Yehuda Ashlag), such as *The Study of the Ten Sefirot* and *The Book of Zohar*. Readers of this book will enjoy the satisfying answers to the riddles of life that only authentic Kabbalah provides. Travel through the pages and prepare for an astonishing journey into the Upper Worlds.

INTRODUCTION TO THE BOOK OF ZOHAR

This volume, along with *The Science of Kabbalah*, is a required preparation for those who wish to understand the hidden message of *The Book of Zohar*. Among the many helpful topics dealt with in this text is an introduction to the "language of roots and branches," without which the stories in *The Zohar* are mere fable and legend. *Introduction to the Book of Zohar* will provide readers with the necessary tools to understand authentic Kabbalah as it was originally meant to be—as a means to attain the Upper Worlds.

THE BOOK OF ZOHAR: ANNOTATIONS TO THE ASHLAG COMMENTARY

The Book of Zohar (*The Book of Radiance*) is an age-old source of wisdom and the basis for all Kabbalistic literature. Since its appearance nearly 2,000 years ago, it has been the primary, and often only, source used by Kabbalists.

For centuries, Kabbalah was hidden from the public, which was deemed not yet ready to receive it. However, our generation has been designated by Kabbalists as the first generation that *is* ready to grasp the concepts in *The Zohar*. Now we can put these principles into practice in our lives.

Written in a unique and metaphorical language, *The Book of Zohar* enriches our understanding of reality and widens our worldview. Although the text deals with one subject only—how to relate to the Creator—it approaches it from different angles. This allows each of us to find the particular phrase or word that will carry us into the depths of this profound and timeless wisdom.

ABOUT BNEI BARUCH

Bnei Baruch is an international group of Kabbalists who share the wisdom of Kabbalah with the entire world. The study materials (in over 30 languages) are authentic Kabbalah texts that were passed down from generation to generation.

HISTORY AND ORIGIN

In 1991, following the passing of his teacher, Rav Baruch Shalom HaLevi Ashlag (The Rabash), Michael Laitman, Professor of Ontology and the Theory of Knowledge, PhD in Philosophy and Kabbalah, and MSc in Medical Bio-Cybernetics, established a Kabbalah study group called "Bnei Baruch." He called it Bnei Baruch (Sons of Baruch) to commemorate his mentor, whose side he never left in the final twelve years of his life, from 1979 to 1991. Dr. Laitman had been Ashlag's prime student and personal assistant, and is recognized as the successor to Rabash's teaching method.

The Rabash was the firstborn son and successor of Rav Yehuda Leib HaLevi Ashlag, the greatest Kabbalist of the 20th century. Rav Ashlag authored the most authoritative and comprehensive commentary on *The Book of Zohar*, titled *The Sulam* (Ladder) *Commentary*. He was the first to reveal the complete method for spiritual ascent, and thus was known as Baal HaSulam (Owner of the Ladder).

Bnei Baruch bases its entire study method on the path paved by these two great spiritual leaders.

THE STUDY METHOD

The unique study method developed by Baal HaSulam and his son, the Rabash, is taught and applied on a daily basis by Bnei Baruch. This method relies on authentic Kabbalah sources such as *The Book of Zohar*, by Rabbi Shimon Bar-Yochai, *The Tree of Life*, by the

Ari, and *The Study of the Ten Sefirot*, by Baal HaSulam.

While the study relies on authentic Kabbalah sources, it is carried out in simple language and uses a scientific, contemporary approach. The unique combination of an academic study method and personal experiences broadens the students' perspective and awards them a new perception of the reality they live in. Those on the spiritual path are thus given the necessary tools to study themselves and their surrounding reality.

Bnei Baruch is a diverse movement of tens of thousands of students worldwide. Students can choose their own paths and intensity of their studies according to their unique conditions and abilities.

THE MESSAGE

The essence of the message disseminated by Bnei Baruch is universal: unity of the people, unity of nations and love of man.

For millennia, Kabbalists have been teaching that love of man should be the foundation of all human relations. This love prevailed in the days of Abraham, Moses, and the group of Kabbalists that they established. If we make room for these seasoned, yet contemporary values, we will discover that we possess the power to put differences aside and unite.

The wisdom of Kabbalah, hidden for millennia, has been waiting for the time when we would be sufficiently developed and ready to implement its message. Now, it is emerging as a solution that can unite diverse factions everywhere, enabling us, as individuals and as a society, to meet today's challenges.

ACTIVITIES

Bnei Baruch was established on the premise that "only by expansion of the wisdom of Kabbalah to the public can we be awarded complete redemption" (Baal HaSulam). Therefore, Bnei Baruch offers a variety of ways for people to explore and discover the purpose of their lives, providing careful guidance for beginners and advanced students alike.

Internet

Bnei Baruch's international website, www.kab.info, presents the authentic wisdom of Kabbalah using essays, books, and original texts. It is by far the most expansive source of authentic Kabbalah material on the Internet, containing a unique, extensive library for readers to thoroughly explore the wisdom of Kabbalah. Additionally, the media archive, www.kabbalahmedia.info, contains thousands of media items, downloadable books, and a vast reservoir of texts, video and audio files in many languages.

Bnei Baruch's online Learning Center offers free Kabbalah courses for beginners, initiating students into this profound body of knowledge in the comfort of their own homes.

Dr. Laitman's daily lessons are also aired live on www.kab.tv, along with complementary texts and diagrams.

All these services are provided free of charge.

Television

In Israel, Bnei Baruch established its own channel, no. 66 on both cable and satellite, which broadcasts 24/7 Kabbalah TV. The channel is also aired on the Internet at www.kab.tv. All broadcasts on the channel are free of charge. Programs are adapted for all levels, from complete beginners to the most advanced.

Conferences

Twice a year, students gather for a weekend of study and socializing at conferences in various locations in the U.S., as well as an annual convention in Israel. These gatherings provide a great setting for meeting like-minded people, for bonding, and for expanding one's understanding of the wisdom.

Kabbalah Books

Bnei Baruch publishes authentic books, written by Baal HaSulam, his son, the Rabash, as well as books by Dr. Michael Laitman. The books of Rav Ashlag and Rabash are essential for complete understanding of the teachings of authentic Kabbalah, explained in Laitman's lessons.

Dr. Laitman writes his books in a clear, contemporary style based on the key concepts of Baal HaSulam. These books are a vital link between today's readers and the original texts. All the books are available for sale, as well as for free download.

Paper

Kabbalah Today is a free paper produced and disseminated by Bnei Baruch in many languages, including English, Hebrew, Spanish, and Russian. It is a political, non-commercial, and written in a clear, contemporary style. The purpose of *Kabbalah Today* is to expose the vast knowledge hidden in the wisdom of Kabbalah at no cost and in a clear, engaging style for readers everywhere.

Kabbalah Lessons

As Kabbalists have been doing for centuries, Laitman gives a daily lesson. The lessons are given in Hebrew and are simultaneously interpreted into seven languages—English, Russian, Spanish, French, German, Italian, and Turkish—by skilled and experienced interpreters. As with everything else, the live broadcast is free of charge.

FUNDING

Bnei Baruch is a non-profit organization for teaching and sharing the wisdom of Kabbalah. To maintain its independence and purity of intentions, Bnei Baruch is not supported, funded, or otherwise tied to any government or political organization.

Since the bulk of its activity is provided free of charge, the prime sources of funding for the group's activities are donations and tithing—contributed by students on a voluntary basis—and Dr. Laitman's books, which are sold at cost.

HOW TO CONTACT
BNEI BARUCH

1057 Steeles Avenue West, Suite 532
Toronto, ON, M2R 3X1
Canada

Bnei Baruch USA
2009 85th street, #51
Brooklyn, New York, 11214
USA

E-mail: info@kabbalah.info
Web site: www.kabbalah.info

Toll free in USA and Canada:
1-866-LAITMAN
Fax: 1-905 886 9697